ANY GIVEN DAY

in the Life of the Bible

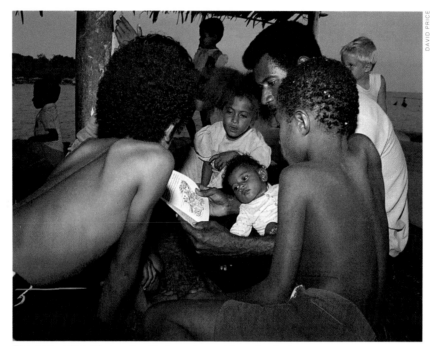

The Ambai ("sea") people of Indonesia read from the first
Scriptures to be translated into their language.

ANY GIVEN DAY

in the Life of the Bible

WYCLIFFE BIBLE TRANSLATORS

MULTNOMAH

Portland, Oregon 97266

Edited by Hyatt Moore
Cover design by Kathy McBride
Cover photo by June Hathersmith
Illustrations by Don Canonge

ANY GIVEN DAY IN THE LIFE OF THE BIBLE
© 1992 by Wycliffe Bible Translators
Published by Multnomah Press
10209 SE Division Street
Portland, Oregon 97266

Multnomah Press is a ministry of
Multnomah School of the Bible
8435 NE Glisan Street
Portland, Oregon 97220

Printed in the United States of America.

Library of Congress Cataloging-in-Publication Data

(CIP data not available at time of printing.)

ISBN 0-88070-513-2

92 93 94 95 96 97 98 99 00 01 - 10 9 8 7 6 5 4 3 2 1

This book is dedicated to
Irwin "Skip" Firchow, Bible
translator, photographer,
artist, gentleman. Skip was to
be one of those working on
this book. However, by
October 1, 1991, having just
returned from a tour of duty in
the South Pacific, Skip was
diagnosed with brain cancer.
He died before the completion
of this book. That, however,
was not before the publication
of his major work—the Rotokas New Testament of Papua
New Guinea. Skip and his
wife, Jackie, with their two
children lived among the Rotokas people on Bougainville
Island over a period of 18
years—learning the language,
building relationships, teaching, and finally, in the translated Scriptures, leaving a legacy
that will survive beyond this
age. We regretted the loss of
Skip's participation on this
project. However, his daughter, Kim Beaty, was one of the
major editors. His son, Steve,
supplied the above illustration.

PHOTOGRAPHERS

Roger Alder
Barb Alvarez
David Andersen
Suree Andersen
Jon Arensen
Glen Bacon
Ruud Bakkar
Ed Beach
Eric Binder
Karen Block
M.B. Borman
Lucia Brubaker
Don Burgess
Merle Busenitz
Denise Campbell
Helja Clouse
Craig Combs
David Crough
Deborah Crough
Jim Daggett
Larry Dodds
Charles Drake
Ken Fast
Kirk Franklin
Dan Garst
Maureen Gerawa
Roy Harris
June Hathersmith
Greg Henderson
Sam Hershberger
Alf Holmen
Don Horneman
Tim Husk
Dan Jore
S.E. Jesudason
Elisabeth Jufer
Steve Kaetterhenry
K.J. Kenfield
Marquita Klaver
Rick Krowchenko
Becky Kelly
Peter Krusi
Constance Kutsch Lojenga
Chris Ladish
Hazel Large

Peter Lawry
Myles Leitch
Floyd Lyon
Kevin Lyon
Bob Mantell
Michael Martens
June Mathias
Rick McArthur
Jim McCauley
Frank McCollum
Sue Newland
David Nicholls
Peter Niesi
Hazel Palileo
Wolfgang Paesler
Jim Parlier
David Pearson
Russ Perry
Rita Peterson
Gunborg Presson
David Price
Marty Quigley
David Ramsdale
Joan Rennie
Gloria Ryan
John Severn
Gwynne Shaver
Jim Skelton
Martin Snook
Ed Speyers
Hugh Steven
Johnny Tenegra
Tom Van Gorkom
Dan Velie
Veli Voipio
Claire Wagner
John Walton
Urs Wegmann
Len Whalley
Fran Woods
Ellen Wroughton
Ritsuko Yamami
Lois Youngman
Jeanne Zaugg
Francis Zurcher

BOOK STAFF

Photo Editor/Manager:	Kirk Franklin
Photography Liaison:	Dave Crough
Associate Editor/Writer:	Kim Beaty
Contributing Writers:	Larry Clark
	Fran Olson
Art Director:	Kathy McBride
Production Assistants:	Ken Harris
	Don Canonge
	Debbie Brown
Publishing Liaison:	W. Terry Whalin
Photographic cataloging:	Nancy Clark
	Theresa Bohm
	Marilyn Laszlo
Editor/Designer:	Hyatt Moore

FOREWORD

October 1 dawned just like any other day. Around the world the same sun came up. With it people rose, fed themselves and moved off into their own variety of endeavors. For certain ones, often in remote and distant places, their endeavors moved another inch toward bringing the Bible to every language. This book is a dawn-to-dusk look at some of what that is all about.

If every photo is worth a thousand words, this book should have some 280,000 words' value. In these pages, you'll get a glimpse of the life of the Bible translator and the team of back-up specialists that supports him or her.

The photos, taken by fellow Wycliffe members, were all shot on a single day, arbitrarily chosen—October 1.

Though the book shows much, a great deal has been left out. Hundreds of other locations where similar work is going on were not photographed. And of those that were covered, only a tiny portion of all that is involved is included. Moreover, nothing of the intangible value is shown at all. Indeed, how can a photograph capture what happens in a life that has laid hold of—or been laid hold of by—the Word of God for the first time?

Some fifty language projects are represented in this book. Over 800 more translations are in progress by Wycliffe linguists. Just as many languages have yet to be entered. Perhaps this book will stimulate beginnings in those. Then, on some other October 1, some year in the future, all the languages in the world will have the Word that God sent for every tongue to know.

Hyatt Moore

In Kenya, Patrick Mangesoy translates Ephesians into his own Sabaot language.

Translation Progress Since the Time of Christ

Ἐν ἀρχῇ ἦν ὁ λόγος, καὶ ὁ λόγος ἦν πρὸς τὸν θεόν, καὶ θεὸς ἦν ὁ λόγος.

"In the beginning was the Word, and the Word was with God, and the Word was God." So begins John's Gospel as written in Greek, above. The Apostle John wrote his Gospel that his readers "might believe that Jesus is the Christ, the Son of God" (John 20:31). He made his case by taking the reader back beyond time to the very beginning and introduced Christ as the Word of God.

Speech is the expression of a man's thoughts and God chose to express his thoughts to us by his speech, or Word. His only Son has made God known to us (John 1:18).

Fortunately, the men who walked with Christ did not keep this Good News to themselves. During the first century they went through the known world declaring that God has made himself known through the Word who became man and had his dwelling among ordinary men (John 1:14).

APOSTLE JOHN

Bible translators in the last 2000 years have appreciated the value of words to express God's thoughts toward man. To make God's Good News available to all people, the first translators put the message into *koine* (common) Greek, the language spoken on the streets throughout the known world.

The Gospel writers were translators. Jesus did not declare his message in Greek, yet his followers used *koine* Greek to convey God's speech in writing. Eight men, Matthew, Mark, Luke, John, Paul, James, Peter and Jude, wrote books of our New Testament to perpetuate the words of Christ and his teachings. Peter declared that the Word of God is imperishable and has the power to bring new life to those who believe its message (1 Peter 1:23).

As the Gospel spread, a number of books (letters) appeared, claiming to have been written by the apostles. To counteract this confusion, several councils were convened during the next two centuries and the 27 New Testament books were acclaimed as having the stamp of authority on them and worthy of attention by Christians everywhere.

JEROME

In the fourth century, Jerome was commissioned by Pope Damasus to translate the New Testament from Greek into Latin. Jerome had lived an ascetic life in the Syrian desert, studying the Scriptures and mastering both Greek and Hebrew. He began his translation in A.D. 382 and two years later moved to Bethlehem where he could continue Hebrew studies for the Old Testament translation. By A.D. 405 he had the entire Bible translated.

Even as the apostles used the common Greek language to express God's message to man, Jerome chose ordinary Latin which was spoken on the streets in his time. His translation of the Bible came to be called the Vulgate, meaning common or usual.

In A.D. 410 the Roman Empire was collapsing and the Roman legions withdrew from their northern colonies. Germanic tribes invaded Celtic Britain and

JOHN WYCLIFFE

over the next few hundred years German dialects vied with Gaelic (still spoken in Ireland, Wales and Scotland). Gradually Anglo-Saxon English evolved and became the language of the courts in England, replacing Latin as the official language.

The church, however, clung to the Latin Vulgate as the only acceptable Scriptures, even though by 1350 sermons were preached and the Bible taught in English to the non-reading masses. In church they heard the Scriptures only in Latin.

An Oxford theologian named John Wycliffe (1330-1380) set about to change this, insisting that the people should have the

Scriptures in their common English language. Wycliffe gathered Oxford scholars around him and they worked together translating the Scriptures. As each portion was translated, Wycliffe had hundreds of handwritten copies made and distributed among the people. Three years after his death his scholar friends finished the translation.

In 1450 Gutenberg revolutionized the world of literature and printing with the invention of movable type. Even though earlier church authorities had opposed Wycliffe's work, now translators began to produce religious works in quantity. Religious books were among the first to be printed. The Hebrew Old Testament appeared in print in 1487 and in 1516 Erasmus published his Greek New Testament. In 1522 Luther finished his translation of the German Bible, which became the foundation for Scriptures in Danish, Swedish, Icelandic and Finnish.

During the 1500s a number of English translations appeared.

A landmark translation was the work of William Tyndale, printed in 1526. His was the first English New Testament based entirely on the original *koine* Greek, and a number of translations that followed were based on Tyndale's work. The Roman Catholic church produced its own English translation of the Bible in 1582, based on Jerome's Latin version, the Vulgate.

WILLIAM TYNDALE

James I (1564-1625), King of England, alarmed by all the versions appearing, commissioned a group of biblical scholars to produce an authorized version, combining the best of earlier translations. The King James Version appeared in 1611, the first Bible produced by an authorized group of scholars.

The Bible, however, was virtually a European book since the majority of Scripture translations were done in languages spoken only in Europe. Missionaries changed that. Matthew's Gospel in Malay appeared in 1629 as the first non-European Scriptures. In America, John Eliot translated the Bible into the language of the Massachusetts Indians. His translation appeared in 1662 and became the first Bible for missionary use in America.

By the 1800s there were 40 languages with whole Bibles and 67 languages with Scripture portions. God used an English cobbler named William Carey to forward translation in India and Asia. Believing the Bible was the most effective way to advance Christianity in areas hostile to the gospel message, Carey translated or helped translate Scripture in over 20 Indian languages, and with his colleagues translated and printed Scripture in 45 languages and dialects in Asia, 35 of these for the first time. All this was done between 1793 and 1834.

Beginning in 1804, Bible societies were formed for the translation, publication and distribution of the Scriptures and translation became a worldwide effort to reach people who had never heard the Good News. In 1818 Luke's Gospel in Tahitian appeared, the first in Oceania. The labor of Marshman, Morrison and Milne resulted in two Chinese Bibles that appeared in 1822 and 1823. The first Scripture published by the Bible Society in Latin America was Luke's Gospel in the Aymara language of Bolivia, spoken today by over a million people.

WILLIAM CAREY

The 1800s also saw two Bibles translated in Africa, the Malagasy Bible of Madagascar (1835), and the Yoruba Bible of Nigeria (1884). The combined population of people speaking these two languages today totals 26,000,000.

Missionary efforts in our twentieth century have resulted in giant leaps forward in Bible translation. In the early twenties a young missionary to the Cakchiquel Indians of Guatemala, W. Cameron Townsend, teamed with an energetic Southern Presbyterian minister and made plans to reach minority languages with the Scriptures. Townsend began his missionary career as a Bible salesman in 1917 but soon discovered that the Mayan Indian groups did not understand Spanish. Townsend turned his attention worldwide when his teammate L.L. Legters toured Brazil in 1926 and returned with a disturbing report: "There must be Indian tribes all over the area, all without the Bible, and precious few missionaries."

Three years after the Cakchiquel New Testament was printed in 1931, Townsend and Legters established Camp Wycliffe, named after the first English Bible translator, and challenged young missionary recruits to make Bible translation their life work. In 1942 these translators organized as Wycliffe Bible Translators (WBT) and the Summer Institute of Linguistics (SIL).

Other translation organizations and Bible societies sprang up and increased efforts to reach the remaining minority languages. Townsend's original cry was "One thousand tongues to go!" until further investigation revealed over 3,000 language groups without the Scriptures.

In 1978 it was thought there were 5,103 languages spoken in the world, but further research has unveiled 1,067 more, for a staggering 6,170, according to *Ethnologue: Languages of the World* (eleventh edition, 1988). Though many of these languages are in dialect families and closely related to each other, nevertheless many are distinct enough to need their own Scripture translation.

CAMERON TOWNSEND

Computers have helped translation progress. However, they cannot replace human creativity and consecration. Of the 6,170 languages in the world today, 827 have a definite need for Scriptures and another 2,495 have a possible need to be determined by further research. Much work is ahead. Many workers are needed.

The *Ethnologue* lists 1157 languages with New Testament translation in progress. The missionary-linguists with Wycliffe Bible Translators and SIL have given New Testaments to over 350 language groups since 1951, when the first Wycliffe translators finished a New Testament for the Highland Mixtec people of Mexico.

We offer praise to God that his divine Word is becoming known to millions of people who have never before had Scriptures in their own tongue.

Dawn, October 1

Give thanks to the Lord,
    Call on his name;
Make known among the nations
    What he has done;
And proclaim that his name is exalted.

ISAIAH 12:4

Sunrise over south-central Texas, where Wycliffe
conducts a training course for missionaries.

● **Previous page:** Dawn tiptoes over northern Kenya (eastern Africa) as Nick and Lynne Swanepoel drive across the desert. They're on a visit to Rendille neighbors, a people for whom they are translating the Scriptures.

Over 50 languages are spoken in the country of Kenya. Some have Scripture portions. Translators are working in others to provide God's Word in the languages the people know best.

● **Above:** The nomadic Rendille people live in stick-and-goatskin "igloos," which they dismantle and load on the camels when it's time to move on.

● **Lower right:** Rendille elders have seen their people suffer ferocious droughts. They know rain brings life. Now they are learning how God's Word is a stream in the desert that brings a new kind of life.

● **Top right:** In southern Kenya, Paul Wyse waits for the sun with a kerosene lamp to push the pre-dawn dark out of his tent. Paul, who is on the staff of a missionary training course, operates his two-way radio as a hobby. Unlike the Rendille, he has had the Bible available to him in his own English language all his life.

BECKY KELLER

EDGAR STEPHEN BEACH

● **Top left:** If you're from Ghana, West Africa, the fire in your clay hearth cooks your breakfast cereal made from ground grain. It ends up a bit like porridge, but with a firmer, gelatinous consistency.

● **Lower left:** In a job where you give a lot, it's pretty important to keep your inner flame burning bright. Wes Collins, Bible translator in Guatemala, tends this fire through his Scripture-reading and personal quiet time. He also uses *Operación Mundo*, the Spanish edition of *Operation World* —a book that lists facts and prayer needs for every country in the world.

Wes has learned both Spanish and the Mam language.

● **Above:** Mr. Coffee, where are you? For that fresh-brewed aroma, Swiss Bible translator Johanna Wegmann pumps the life into this Primus stove to get the burner going.

Johanna and her husband, Urs, live among the Yau people in Papua New Guinea.

In the morning, O Lord, you hear my voice; in the morning I lay my requests before you and wait in expectation.

PSALM 5:3

● **Above and inset:** When the heat is right, Wes Shoemaker in Mexico pops on the tortillas— what everyone eats around here. Wes ground the corn for these tortillas and made them himself.

Wes and his wife, Julie, were translators in Papua New Guinea when their son contracted a mosquito-borne virus called blackwater fever. Doctors told them they needed to move to a country where their son couldn't contract it again. They moved to Tucson, Arizona, far from disease-bearing mosquitoes.

They translate for the Tarahumara people who live below the border in Chihuahua state, Mexico.

● **Far right:** Meanwhile in Alaska, it's sub-zero weather outside. Inside, Dave and Mitzi Shinen start the day with quiet time together—but not before Dave prepares his shower—the do-it-yourself kind.

Dave and Mitzi Shinen translate among the Yupik Eskimos, half of whom live in Siberia and half in Alaska, mostly on St. Lawrence Island in the Bering Sea. For over 40 years, the Cold War kept the Yupiks apart. In 1989, three walrus-skin boats full of Siberian Yupiks were allowed to cross the 38 miles of sea to St. Lawrence Island. They left a month later with booklets of John and Jude in Yupik.

HUGH STEVEN

Above: Translator Doug Towne and son Timothy, in Zacatepec, Mexico, wait for their fresh-squeezed orange juice. As Paul walked down the street, he visited with local friends along the way. This kind of contact is what the broader picture of Bible translation is all about: touching lives and building relationships.

Right: On the island of Sulawesi, Indonesia, a pet hornbill gets his tasty breakfast of ripe papaya.

Opposite: Coffee is a cash crop on Sulawesi and also a favorite local beverage, drunk strong and black and laced with sugar.

On this island, languages spoken number 105. Less then a quarter have translated Scriptures.

MICHAEL MARTEN

Oh, Dad, when do we eat? Little Timothy Towne is ready to dig in. The bowl contains *barbacoa* (goat meat), a common local menu item, purchased from a street vendor.

The Towne family regularly prays for colleagues and friends, using a small notebook filled with picture prayer cards.

After he shot this picture, photographer Hugh Steven sat down at the empty place setting to enjoy fresh squeezed orange juice, scrambled eggs and goat meat.

HUGH STEVEN

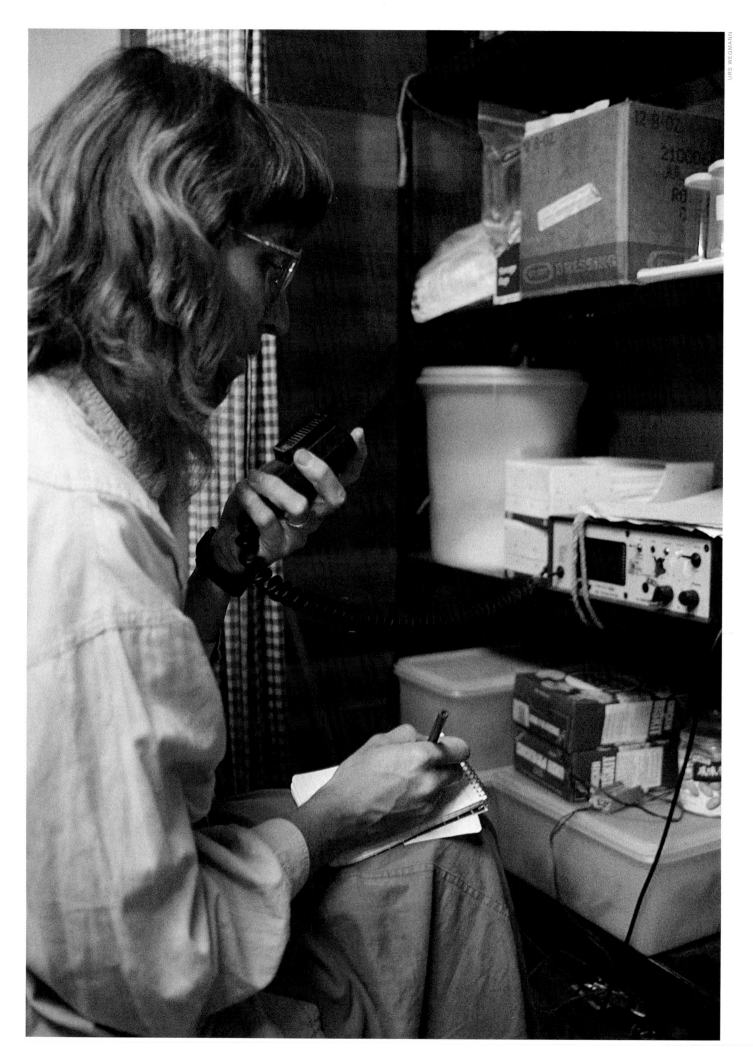

Left: "72 Charlie Uniform, this is 42 Echo X-ray. Do you read? Over." Johanna Wegmann in Papua New Guinea speaks with the radio operator at the SIL work center in the highlands. Two-way radios are crucial tools for field workers in areas with limited or no telephone service.

Right: Pilot Bob Boogaard pulls the Piper Navajo out from the hangar in Lomalinda, Colombia, to prepare for the day's flights.

Right, below: Translators Ismo and Judith Routamaa from Finland depend on planes and pilots to carry their family to the Papua New Guinean village where they work.

JAARS (formerly Jungle Aviation and Radio Service) provides technical and business personnel to serve Wycliffe translators in areas such as aviation and communications.

21

CHARLES DRAKE

● **Above:** A woman of Bongao Island in the Philippines gathers sea creatures for her breakfast.

● **Top right:** A sailboat with outboard motor chugs quietly across a still Ambon Bay. In the Maluku Islands of Indonesia, once called the Spice Islands, 133 languages are spoken. Translators are working to bring God's Word to the people that speak these languages.

FRANK McCOLLUM

RUSS PERRY

FRANK MCCOLLUM

● **Left:** Scripture translation begins with language learning. You do that by merging with the lives of those who speak the language. British translator Carrie Beckley in Indonesia takes advantage of the community dishwashing time to learn the difference between the words "washing" and "scrubbing."

● **Far left:** Later, Carrie buys smoked tuna for the Indonesian family she lives with. Shopping for groceries is her regular "chore," providing daily opportunities to practice the language in this commerce context.

Following page: The Yora Indians of Peru use hammocks as beds by night and easy-chairs by day. Until 1985, no outsiders had been able to contact this group. When a pneumonia and malaria epidemic began to ravage their people, three Yoras ventured out of the jungles, found a Wycliffe translator and pilot, and asked for help. A medical team traveled to the isolated area and treated over 200 Yoras. This contact led to the Yoras inviting Wycliffe workers to come and translate the Scriptures for them.

PETER LAWRY

LEN WHALLEY

26

HUGH STEVEN

On any given day in Bible translation, scenes like these occur around the world.

● **Top left:** In Indonesia, Dave Price and Bernard Paisei translate Luke into the Ambai language.

● **Left:** David Crawford and Graham Kulyuru in South Australia check literacy books in the Pitjantjatjara language spoken by Aborigines.

● **Above:** In Mexico, Doug and Linda Towne and co-translator Pascual work on their personal journals. They write in Zacatepec as a language exercise to prepare them for translation work later in the morning.

● **Right**: Translator Ed Robinson studies the Thai language with tutor Suraphon Watana in Bangkok, Thailand.

KAREN BLOCK

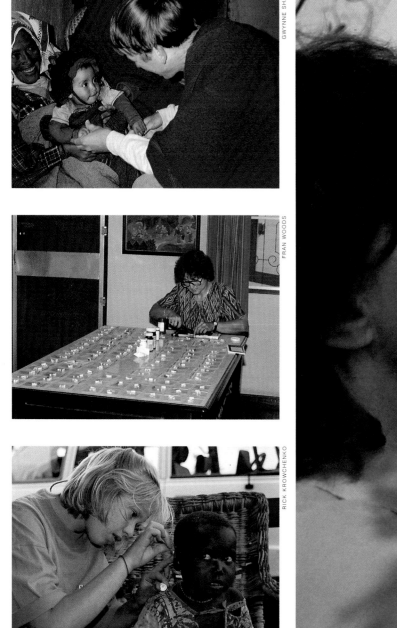

GWYNNE SHAVER

FRAN WOODS

RICK KROWCHENKO

Bible translation means much more than parking at a desk, churning out paper and leaving a book ten or twenty years later. It means giving time—to talk, to learn, to minister—to those you live among. It's when you care for the whole person, mind, body and soul that your gospel speaks.

● **Large photo:** In Kenya, Lynne Swanepoel treats a Rendille woman with mouth sores. Lynne's compassion has been developed through her life experiences, which include a ministry years ago to inner-city drug addicts.

● **Left, top:** In Peru, Bible translator Dwight Shaver checks a Quechua baby. Dwight grew up in Peru and followed in his translator parents' footsteps.

*And he healed those that had
need of healing.*

LUKE 9:11

● **Left, middle:** Some workers fight health limitations as they carry out demanding jobs. Paulette Hopple in Thailand struggles with a lung condition that makes breathing difficult and saps her strength. Medication and vitamins, which she sorts here, give her a good measure of stability.

● **Left, bottom:** In Kenya, ten-year-old Elise, daughter of Bible translators Jim and Henny Leonard, treats a Sabaot girl for an ear-infection. Elise always prays with her patients before they leave.

● **Above, right:** In Ecuador, Ron Borman inspects a boil he has lanced. Ron grew up in this area while his parents, Bub and Bobbie, translated the Scriptures into the Cofan language.

After a 600-year dorman- cy, in June 1991 the Phil- ippines' Mt. Pinatubo erupted, spewing two bil- lion tons of ash into the air. This settled onto the land below, its accumulated weight crushing homes and burying villages.

Over 300,000 people fled the area or were evacuated before the eruption. Most were Aytas, semi-nomadic for- est-dwellers. They settled in "tent cities" set up by the Philippine Govern- ment and Red Cross.

Wycliffe field workers such as Roger Green, who speaks the Ayta Mag- Indi dialect, helped in the relief efforts.

PHOTOS: JOHN WALTON

Since Bible translation involves meeting the needs of the whole person, disaster situations present many opportunities for Wycliffe workers to show care and concern. When the Ayta people were displaced to the tent cities, language workers in the Philippines helped provide supplies, including rice cooking pots.

Large photo: Tent cities such as Nueva Ecija housed between 1,000 and 5,000 refugees.

Left inset: At Nueva Ecija, a structure of local materials takes shape for a pre-school for refugee kids.

Middle inset: Ayta mom with her one-week-old baby and son.

Right inset: Bible Translator Roger Green provides school supplies for pre-school teachers at Nueva Ecija. Before the eruption, Roger and wife Joanne conducted a pre-school for Ayta kids in their own language.

33

*He guides the humble in what is right and teaches
them his way. All the ways of the Lord are loving
and faithful. . . .*

PSALM 25:9, 10

● **Left:** The bilingual school in Comitancillo, Guatemala, is highly successful. Children such as this young girl learn to read and write in their own language before tackling studies in Spanish, which they must also learn later on.

● **Below:** This bilingual sign reveals the pride the Indian people have in their own language. It reads, "Welcome to Comitancillo."

Before Bible translators worked with the Mam people to devise an alphabet, billboards like this weren't even possible.

● **Overleaf:** Pilots never know what they might encounter on rural grass airstrips. In Peru, Floyd Lyon scans the flight board with warnings about local airstrips.

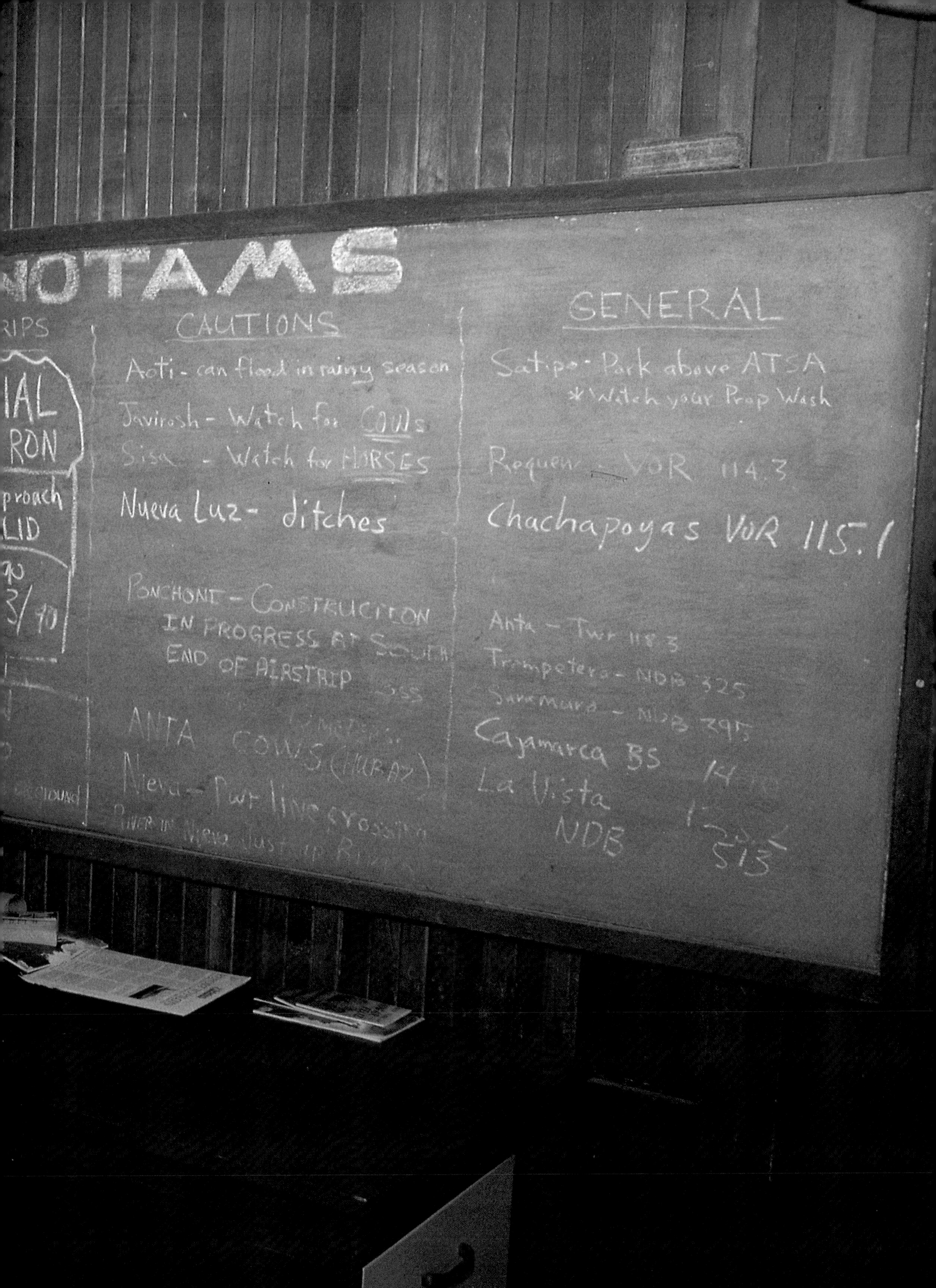
NOTAMS
CAUTIONS
Aoti - can flood in rainy season
Javirosh - Watch for COWS
Sisa - Watch for HORSES
Nueva Luz - ditches
PONCHONI - CONSTRUCTION IN PROGRESS AT SOUTH END OF AIRSTRIP
ANTA COWS
GENERAL
Satipo - Park above ATSA
* Watch your Prop Wash
Chachapoyas VOR 115.1
Anta - Twr 118.3
Cajamarca BS
La Vista
NDB
513

Top: Yann Kabai is one of a growing number of translators around the world working to provide Scriptures in their own language. At his home in Samel Village (Papua New Guinea), Yann translates Luke into his Biliau language. He'll take this first draft and check it with a committee comprising local Biliau men and women and a translator/advisor from Wycliffe. Yann received training through a National Translators course and is sponsored by his village church.

Left: During World War II, Papua New Guinea saw lots of action. Rusted-out war materiel now lies strewn across the islands, providing play spots for kids.

Large photo: Since that war, airstrips have been built all over the country. Today, Bible translators and literacy workers in Papua New Guinea are flown by missionary pilots to remote locations in airplanes or helicopters.

KIRK FRANKLIN

You will go out in joy and be led forth in peace; the mountains and hills will burst into song before you, and all the trees of the field will clap their hands.

ISAIAH 55:12

LARRY DODDS

GUNBORG PRESSON

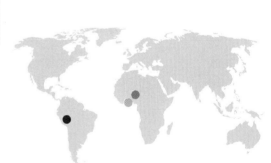

Left: Smoke from a cooking fire inside the house of Bible translators Kim and Carolyn Fowler mingles with dissipating morning fog in southern Peru. The pilot of the airplane just spent the night with them—a not uncommon event where fog closes in or darkness comes too soon. This plane isn't equipped for night flying by instrument.

Below, left: It's always an exciting day when a translator holds in her hands the product of many years' labor! Eva Flik peruses a Dan New Testament, part of a shipment that's just arrived in Côte d'Ivoire (West Africa). Eva (from Germany) and her Swiss co-worker, Margrit Bolli, have simultaneously worked on three New Testament translations. The Dan is the first of the three to be completed.

Right: Mail call! As God's letter is translated and delivered to the world, it's letters from family and friends back home that encourage and brighten the day for field workers.

Below: Burkina Faso in West Africa is a hot, dry country, prone to drought and famine. Water is a precious commodity, used carefully. Seventy-two languages are spoken in this country of over seven million people. Half of those languages have no Scriptures.

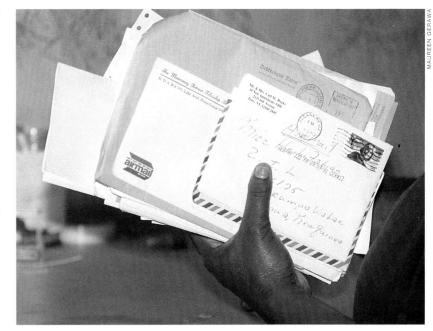

Graphic artists. Audio technicians. Writers. Video producers. What do they have to do with Bible translation? Everything.

● **Top, near right:** In Guatemala, audio technician Miguel Rocche (in white shirt) guides Octavio Ramirez in recording Scripture stories in the Mam language onto cassette. With translated Scriptures on tape, people who can't read yet can still hear God's Word.

● **Top, middle:** Technician Tony Gorsline, about to be eaten by Wycliffe Canada's encroaching video equipment. The Media Department produces videos that explain Bible translation and attempt to challenge the Christian public to get involved.

● **Top, far right:** Kathryn Dodds Moore, writer in Peru, picks slides to accompany an article. Writers tell of the needs, progress and results of literacy and Bible translation. Their reports inform host-country leaders, and their stories are published in brochures, letters and publications that update and encourage prayer and financial partners back home.

● **Bottom, near right:** Peter Cox works on a video that tells Australian pastors and churches about Bible translation.

● **Bottom, middle:** Graphic artists such as Kamal Gideon in Singapore design Wycliffe publications to be effective, professional and eye-catching.

● **Bottom, far right:** To stir interest in translated Scripture and promote Scripture distribution, technicians in Guatemala have dubbed Mayan language narration onto videos of the "Jesus" film and the New Media Bible. Here Manuel Chávez works at a mixing board.

Each one should use whatever gift he has received to serve others, faithfully administering God's grace in its various forms.

1 PETER 4:10

KEN FAST

DAN VELIE

S.E. JESUDASON

MARTY QUIGLEY

● **Overleaf:** At the translation table: Urs Wegmann (from Switzerland) and co-workers discuss a translated portion of Scripture in the Yau language of Papua New Guinea. The walls of the study are bamboo, split, spread flat and woven in a common stair-step pattern.

URS WEGMANN

Right: Veteran linguist and Nobel Peace Prize-nominee Ken Pike shares some wisdom with Wycliffe USA Director Hyatt Moore.

Far right: Bible translation on a worldwide scale means global and strategic planning. Administrators look at all kinds of elements, from training to funding to national involvement to work methods in sensitive countries. At the international headquarters in Dallas, Texas, key leaders review training programs for Bible translators, literacy specialists and support workers. Clockwise from Bernie May (speaking): Roger Gilstrap, Dr. Bob Dooley, Dr. Ray Gordon, Dr. Des Derbyshire, Dr. John Bendor-Samuel, Dr. Frank Robbins, Dr. Jim Holsclaw, Dr. David Bendor-Samuel.

Below: In Ecuador, Bible translator Neil Wiebe compares Chachi words with words in Colorado, a related language.

Below right: Manabu Ishikawa in Wycliffe's Japan office in Tokyo. Like a number of Wycliffe offices around the world, Japan's operates with a minimal staff, who usually carry separate part- or full-time jobs. But they're dedicated to Bible translation and work to challenge their Christian countrymen to become involved.

WOLFGANG PAESLER

Above: Move over, Mr. Universe. Teacher Volker Scharpe and friend Destin Leon work out in Côte d'Ivoire (West Africa). Volker has come from Germany to teach children of German missionaries. Destin is a Bible translation co-worker.

Top right: Pushing off for a Sunday cruise? Not exactly. Rocky shores and surging seas make it quite a production to go to and from tiny Mota Island in the South Pacific Republic of Vanuatu. Bible translator Dan Garst helps friends Tony, Jenkins and Dean get on their way. Motorboat is the only way to get on and off the island, unless you like swimming through waters inhabited by sharks. Field workers who live on islands across the Pacific accept open-sea travel as part of the package, but it can cause special anxiety as they consider the safety of their families.

Right: River travel is somewhat less stressful, unless you're in a tippy canoe with a less-than-refined sense of balance! Young Daniel Leitch, son of translators Myles and Janet, is at home among his Babole friends in the Congo (Central Africa).

MYLES LEITCH

They were glad when it grew calm, and he guided them to their desired haven.

PSALM 107:30

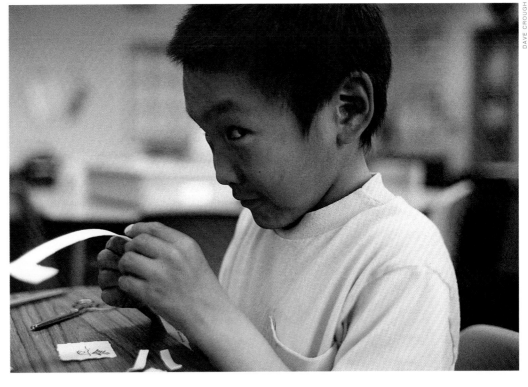

DAVE CROUGH

DAVE CROUGH

● **Left:** In 1971, the Alaskan government passed laws that directed its schools to teach native Alaskan languages. The University of Alaska Linguistics Department asked SIL's help. For the next six years, Dave Shinen and wife Mitzi developed Yupik textbooks and reading materials and trained Yupik Eskimos to be language instructors. The result is an extensive library of Yupik literacy materials and effective bilingual schools.

● **Top and above:** One such school is Gambell Elementary. Here kids learn to read and write in their Yupik language before learning in English. This preparation will result in young readers ready for the Yupik Scriptures.

When field workers go to other countries, they often face enormous differences in language, culture and lifestyle. New personnel attend training courses in or near the country where they will work.

Above: On "Kenya Safari," one such course in Africa, Director Jon Arensen and staff lecture on topics ranging from health care to spiritual warfare.

Below: Participants camp near the land of the Maasai people. A junior camper watches Maasai-owned cattle.

Above left: Seasoned field personnel staff the training courses. John Ottaviano, lecturing at the Americas Field Training Course in Texas, translated the Scriptures into the Tacana language of Bolivia. Jon Arensen grew up in Tanzania and worked on the Murle translation in Sudan.

JON ARENSEN

LARRY DODDS

Sickness strikes hard among the Yora people of Peru. In this case, the babies and children are the sufferers.

Below and top left:
Here on the front porch of Bible translators Kim and Carolyn Fowler's house in Potaya village, Yora parents have brought their children for help.

PETE LAWRY

LARRY DODDS

PETE LAWRY

Middle left: Carolyn talks to the family of a dying baby whose sickness turned into pneumonia. Visiting for two days to take pictures for this book, Dr. Larry Dodds treated the baby and other sick children. Despite the antibiotics he administered, the baby died (**lower left**), its case of pneumonia too advanced to respond to treatment. Here the father grieves for his child.

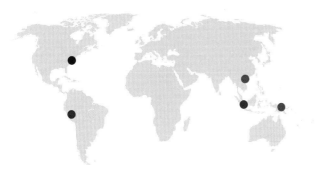

Where would field workers be without wings? Probably longer in years and the worse for wear. They'd have to hike over peak and plain to reach some of the places where they work. And others, on far-flung islands, couldn't get there at all.

JAARS, Wycliffe's technical and business arm, operates over 45 aircraft worldwide specifically to speed Bible translation and serve the host countries. Every year, pilots collectively fly some 1.8 million miles, cart around 36,500 passengers and transport 4.6 million pounds of cargo.

People will come from east and west and north and south, and will take their places at the feast in the kingdom of God.

LUKE 13:29

● **Far left:** It all starts here at the JAARS center near Charlotte, North Carolina. On the hangar floor, aircraft mechanics and technicians overhaul a wing for a DC-3 destined for Africa. All pilots go through training conducted by veteran field aviators, to prepare them for the challenges of overseas conditions like short, uphill airstrips that end in drop-offs. . . .

● **Top left:** In Indonesia, Pat Andrews hugs little Claire goodbye just before he boards the twin-engine Piper Aztec that will take him to Halmahera Island. After the two-hour flight, Pat has a one-hour bus ride and a 24-hour boat trip to take to reach Buli village to do linguistic survey.

● **Lower left:** Aviation mechanic Mark Ott checks the engine of a Helio 1188 in Peru. During a morning flight, the oil overheated, and Mark is trying to find out why.

○ **Top middle:** In Brazil, pilot Douglas Baughman confers with a bevy of Nadeb Indians on how to get his Cessna 206 out of there! (Or so it looks.)

● **Lower middle:** Aviation mechanic Dave Immel in Papua New Guinea removes a rebuilt engine from the test stand to install in a Cessna 206.

● **Top right:** Little planes are the workhorses that carry field personnel. Most of SIL's single-engine and small twin-engine aircraft can seat three to five passengers, depending on the amount of cargo.

● **Lower right:** In Singapore a Turbine Pilatus-Normen Britten is refurbished before being ferried for use in Papua New Guinea.

10:00 A.M.

● **Above:** Inchuchu Sirayon splashes color against the desert as he hangs up wet clothes in Kenya, eastern Africa.

● **Right, top and bottom:** Nick Swanepoel and co-translators produce a newspaper in the Rendille language of Kenya. It covers topics from camel care and health to literacy. Besides the practical help, it provides practice in reading and promotes literature as a cultural value.

With two Rendille warriors, Nick shows the latest issue to the owner of a small store.

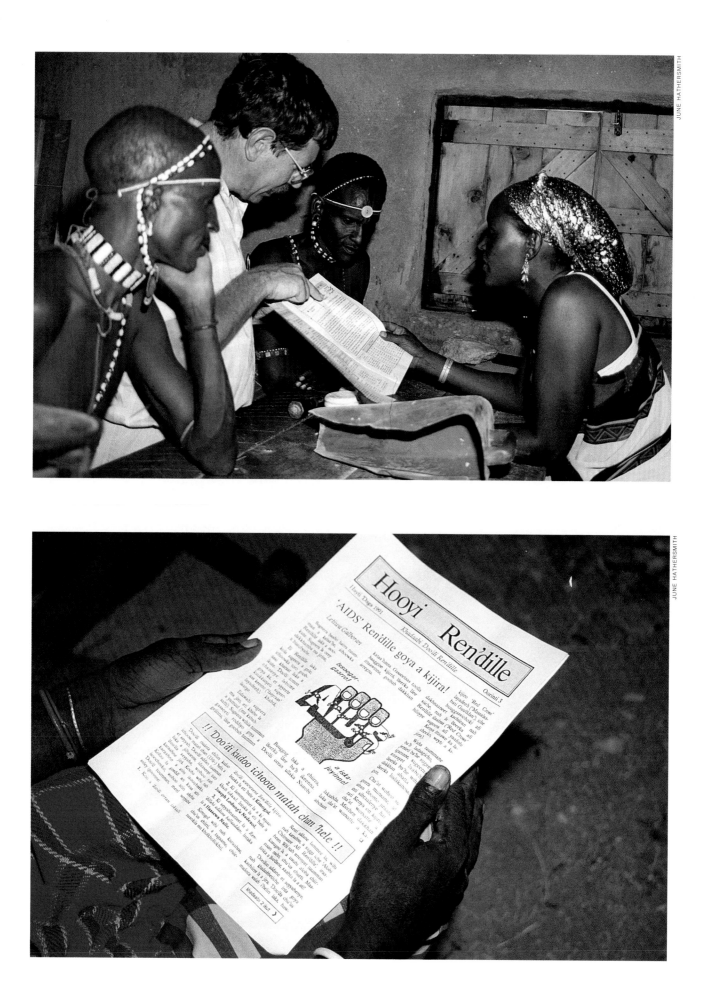

CHARLES DRAKE

FRANCIS ZURCHER

● **Top:** Sama speakers in a traditional dance on the shore of Bongao Island in the Philippines.

● **Above:** Parlez vous francais? Most field workers destined for West Africa must learn French, since it's the national language in many countries. The "Inlingua" school in Switzerland provides French courses 12 to 18 months long. They're intense: you eat, sleep and nightmare in French!

● **Right:** "Hey, Jennifer, wanna hear a secret?" Jennifer and Nathan Garst live with their parents on Mota, a tiny island in Vanuatu in the South Pacific. The Garsts are translating with a committee of local Christians in Mariu village.

JIM PARLIER

DEBORAH CROUGH

Previous page:
Celebrate life! Lynne
Swanepoel shares a
timeless moment of
laughter and friendship
with Rendille women in
eastern Africa.

JUNE HATHERSMITH

The man who plants and the man who waters have one purpose, and each will be rewarded according to his own labor.

1 CORINTHIANS 3:8

HAZEL LARGE

Wycliffe Associates (WA), the lay ministry of Wycliffe Bible Translators, supports and encourages Bible translation in practical ways. Volunteers use their skills in hands-on projects and form local chapters to get people interested in and praying for worldwide translation work. WA construction staff design and build Wycliffe facilities. (Architect Tony James, **far left;** Steve Cowles, **left,** at new administrative building in Dallas, Texas).

Above: WA builds facilities internationally. In England, volunteers built a library for students preparing for Bible translation.

Computers have enabled translators to produce more consistent and thorough translations, as well as dialect adaptations and non-Roman characters. Computer personnel such as Jim Albright in Brazil provide essential technical help.

Computers and Bible Translation

Top: Bible translator David Payne with co-worker Samuel, in Peru, working on the Ashénin-ca Campa Scriptures.

Middle: Mary Smith shows Dr. Zakaria Fadoul, a linguist at the University of N'Djamena (Cameroon, West Africa), how to use a program that analyzes speech sounds.

Below: In Papua New Guinea, Douglas Bennett with translation checking committee makes refine-ments on the Yamai Scriptures using a Toshi-ba computer.

Next page

Top left: Mary Cates enters prayer requests and praise items from Wycliffe workers all over the world. This list is mailed to those who have committed to pray for Bible translation work.

Middle left: In England, Trevis Gosling tends to the accounting for Wyc-liffe Europe.

Missionary linguists have taken full advantage of the computer age to advance Bible translation around the world. Gone are the days when translators stored valuable language data on file cards and typed sheet after sheet of translated Scriptures.

With computers the translator does mundane tasks quickly and the finished text of a translation goes directly to a type-setter for printing of a New Testament book. Also the mis-sionary can finish one translation and then use the computer to assist another translation in a related language.

In one case, it took Bob and Jo Ann Conrad ten years to finish the Mufian New Testament in Papua New Guinea, but they expect to finish in two years the New Testament in the related Filifita language. With the help of a tiny Sharp PC-5000, they have adapted the Mufian New Testament text into Filifita and then checked the print-outs with speakers of the language.

A problem arises when languages are not closely related. Over 14 million people speak Quechua in South America but these modern descendants of the ancient Incas have spread out over Peru, Ecuador and Bolivia. Today, there are at least 25 dialects so distinct that those in one region can barely un-derstand Quechuas from another region.

Computer linguists have devised a program that takes a translation printed in one area and adapts the text to another dialect. Even translators without advanced computer train-ing can use the program with only a laptop computer.

Computers also help the translator who is studying a tonal language. When tones and accents change the meaning of words, the translator needs an extra set of ears. The compu-ter is attached to a speech analysis machine and then it reproduces the sounds in graphic form, much like a heart-graphing machine would monitor a heartbeat.

Another 1000 languages still do not have Scriptures and some of these languages in Africa and Asia use non-Roman script. For example, the Tai Dam of Vietnam use three ornate scripts, each vastly different. In the past, language materials for the Tai Dam people have been written by hand in the Tai Dam script and then typed on manual typewriters in the Lao-tian and Vietnamese scripts, a slow and laborious process.

Computers now speed the typing, editing and revision of New Testaments with non-Roman scripts. The final edited copy of a New Testament can be transferred to a photo type-setter for printing. All of these advances in technology give translators greater efficiency and accuracy in their work.

With all this technology, however, there is no substitute for human ingenuity and consecration. One computer whiz who is also a Christian says, "The computer may help us do the job faster, better and in a more enjoyable working envi-ronment, but it can't show God's love. That's where the real translation takes place."

Below: In Guatemala, a computer has adapted the Central Cakchiquel translation to produce an initial draft in the Western Cakchiquel language.

Top right: Although Wycliffe operates state-of-the-art computer equipment, magnetic tape is still used to transfer stored information to companies that only accept such tape. In North Carolina, Doug Demick removes a tape.

Right, upper middle: Avelino Yaxon keyboards translated Western Cakchiquel Scriptures in Guatemala.

Right: Francisco Orozco helps Wes Shoemaker learn the Central Tarahumara language of Mexico.

Bottom right: James Githukah, Literacy Coordinator for the national Bible translation organization in Kenya, uses a computer in planning literacy programs.

When folks work overseas, they need folks back home taking care of the business. . . .

Many home teams are small—like Wycliffe Netherlands (**below**, Helma Rem), with under a dozen staff members. Some are large. Wycliffe USA consists of 250 workers in the California office (**large photo**) and more staff in six regional offices.

Like field workers, Wycliffe home missionaries receive no guaranteed salary. They look to God to supply their needs through friends and churches. And like field workers, they fill critical roles in the work of Bible translation. Some

RUUD BAKKER

CLAIRE WAGNER

ROGER ALDER

CLAIRE WAGNER

process checks from financial partners. Some recruit teachers for field workers' kids. Others maintain health care and retirement plans. Whether in accounting (**bottom left**, Wycliffe Australia), art, computer programming, or advising members on furlough plans (**middle, left,** Wycliffe USA), all play an important part on the home team.

Rendille warriors wait, as silent as the thorn trees that puncture this eastern Africa desert.

Inset: This isn't an afternoon gossip group. These Rendille women, many of whom have lost children to disease, are eager to learn the basics of first aid and preventive medicine. Bible translator Lynne Swanepoel hopes to train one woman in every Rendille village who will then pass on the learning.

12:00 NOON

12:30 P.M.

Bible translation is not accomplished by waltzing into a country uninvited and setting up shop. Rather, Wycliffe translators work in cooperation with government leaders, securing invitations to carry out linguistic work, literacy and Bible translation. Building and maintaining good relations with host country leaders can mean the difference between "Stay" and "Close the door on your way out."

Top left: In Quito, Ecuador, Public Relations Director Roy Peterson places name cards in preparation for a dinner with government leaders who will receive translated publications.

Bottom left: Roy waits to greet the special guests outside the restaurant.

Below: The event in full swing.

I urge, then, that requests, prayers . . . and thanksgiving be made for everyone—for kings and all those in authority, that we may live peaceful and quiet lives.

1 TIMOTHY 2:1,2

RITA PETERSON

1:00 P.M.

Left and below: While we might collapse in ecstasies over a chocolate eclair, to the Pitjantjatjara Aborigines of Australia, a nice, fresh Wichiti grub calls forth the same response. Bible translator Jan Crawford and friend Kanytjupai have searched under the Ilykuwara bush, where Wichiti grubs hide in the roots. They found several, which Jan let Kanytjupai enjoy.

Right: Speaking of lunch: students at the Asia Summer Institute of Linguistics school in Singapore take a break from studies. This school serves students from Asian nations including Malaysia, South Korea, Indonesia, Japan, Hong Kong and India. Students receive training in literacy work, applied linguistics and translation, preparing them to be Bible translators.

S.E. JESUDASON

Overleaf: These men who speak the Mam language are bound for sugar-cane farms on Guatemala's coast. The income they earn will help provide for their families' needs.

EDGAR STEPHEN BEACH

HUGH STEVEN

● **Above:** A translated Bible isn't much use if people don't know how to read.

Linda Towne in Mexico writes reading primers, plans reading lessons and develops stories in the Zacatepec Mixteco language. Then she takes the stories to friends such as Maria to test for reading ability and understanding.

● **Below:** After a full morning's work, linguist Duane Clouse in Indonesia gets horizontal for a few minutes.

● **Right:** In Indonesia, daughter Lalita joins the fun as her dad, Australian David Andersen, curls his tongue around some Moronene words. Language-learning takes time and practice.

HELJA CLOUSE

"There is a time for everything, and a season for every activity under heaven."

ECCLESIASTES 3:1

There are different kinds of gifts, but the same Spirit. There are different kinds of service, but the same Lord.

1 CORINTHIANS 12:4, 5

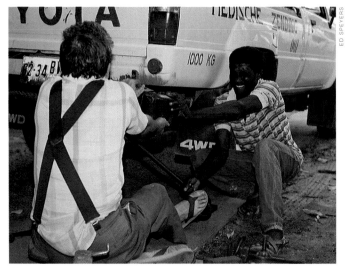

● Bub Catlett and co-worker maintain vehicles used by field personnel in Suriname, South America.

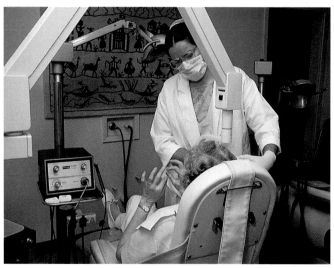

● Everyone gets cavities! Dental assistant Mary Troyer helps volunteer dentists treat Wycliffe patients at the California home office.

● Mike Matthews rivets the wing of a Helio Courier airplane in the northern Philippines.

● Without humor, we'd be dull people! In Colombia, Ray Rising may not be able to breathe, but he does a great job repairing a communication service monitor.

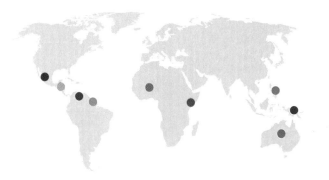

MARTY QUIGLEY

● Rafael Herrera runs a Heidelberg press in the SIL printshop in Guatemala City. He prints literature, primers and Scriptures.

JUNE MATHIAS

● Swiss construction and maintenance technician Andreas Eichenberger installs a ground wire in Burkina Faso, West Africa.

MERLE BUSENITZ

● Third-year apprentice Ave Serave greases a nose steering bearing on an airplane in Papua New Guinea.

STEVE KAETTERHENRY

● British maintenance technician Martin Parkes welds a utility trailer in Australia.

● **Overleaf:** Every 14 years, the Rendille men of eastern Africa choose one young man to be set apart for a special position of service. His job is simply to meet whatever needs he sees.

On this day, the camels required watering, so he stepped in to help. He waters them from a deep, ancient well chiselled out of stone.

JUNE HATHERSMITH

Five-photo sequence, right: In Ecuador, South America, Cofan pottery-making has traditionally been a woman's job. Elvira, who is firing the pots, plates and griddles, learned the art from her mother and is passing it on to her granddaughters. She uses split bamboo, which burns hot and fast, to fire the pottery.

12:30 P.M.

12:40 P.M.

12:45 P

1:20 P.M.

1:30 P.M.

Far left: Bub Borman and Leoncio Aguinda check their translation of an Old Testament abridgment in the Cofan language of Ecuador. Bub and his wife, Bobbie, have worked among the Cofan people since 1955. The New Testament translation was dedicated in 1980.

Left: Anaseto Quenamá and Locrecia Queta, Cofan friends, are a special couple to the Bormans, since their granddaughter married Bub and Bobbie's son.

DAN JORE

Large photo: Vast reaches of rainforest march across Brazil, divided occasionally by waterways such as the Madeira. Over 200 languages are spoken by people living under the forest's canopy.

Far left: Wycliffe personnel govern themselves by an electoral system. They choose a director and an executive committee, who serve for specific terms and afterward return to their original jobs. The Brazil Executive Committee meets with Director John Taylor (**left**).

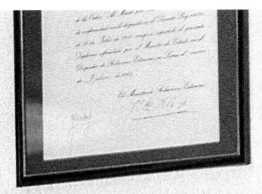
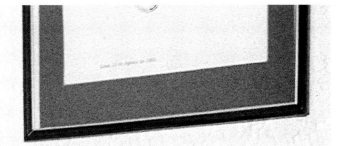

In North Carolina, a portrait of Wycliffe founder William Cameron Townsend and his wife, Elaine, hangs among 21 awards presented to him by various international government leaders for work in Bible translation, literacy and bilingual education.

Joyce Gullman straightens a certificate of honor called "El Sol del Peru."

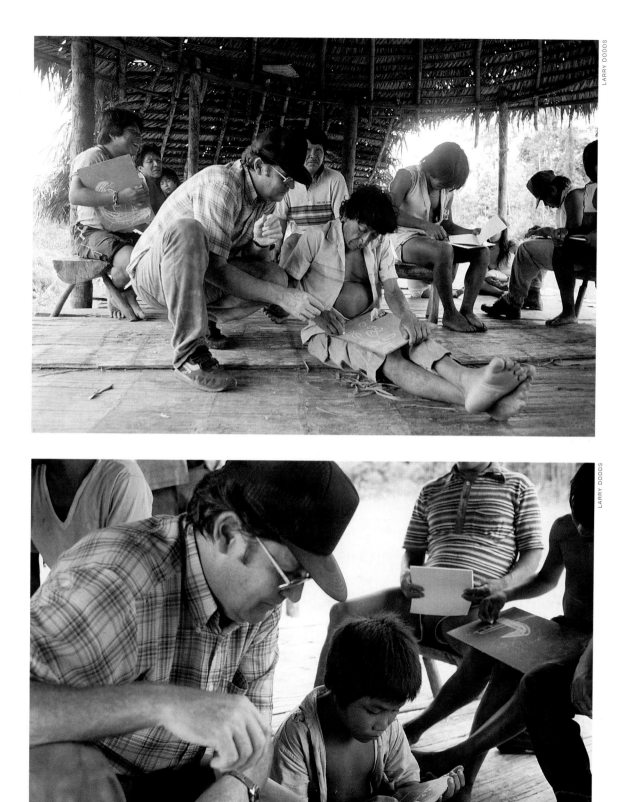

LARRY DODDS

LARRY DODDS

● Literacy means one can read dosages on medicine bottles, land-rights papers, health booklets and God's Word. In Peru, Shipibo kids (**left**) get a head start and Kim Fowler (**above**) teaches reading to Yora Indians.

The literacy effort among the Yoras is just beginning. A community school was built recently, and Kim and his wife, Carolyn, have started reading classes.

Learning to read will give the Yora Indians—who only number about 200—a critical tool for their survival as a distinct people.

● **Left:** In Peru, translator Carolyn Fowler guides a Yora Indian boy in a writing drill.

● **Below:** In Ecuador, Sivivico beetles dry in the sun. The Cofan people remove the irridescent wings and string them together to make vivid, sparkling necklaces.

● **Far right, top:** Previously known as Auca ("savage") by the outside world, the Waorani Indians of Ecuador inspect print styles, pictures and covers of sample books to help them decide how their New Testament should look. One of the men who participated in killing the five missionaries in 1956 helped make the selection. The printed New Testament reached them in the summer of 1992.

● **Far right, bottom:** Esther Borman gets measured for a dress by Severina Auenama. Esther and husband Ron work in the Cofan area of Ecuador, where Ron was raised as the son of Bible translators.

M.B. BORMAN

M.B. BORMAN

PETER NIESI

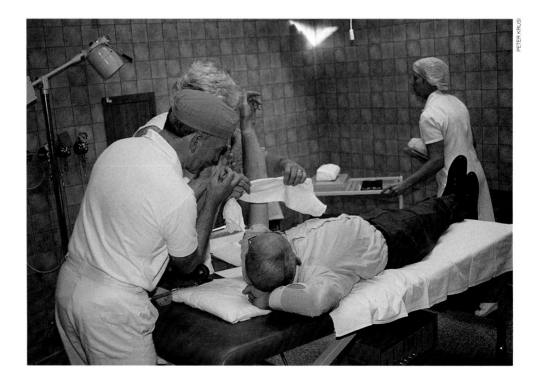

PETER KRUSI

● **Above:** Sometimes God takes people trained in nurturing physical life to nurture spiritual life as well. Australian medical doctor David Lithgow has been involved in the translation of New Testaments in three separate languages in Papua New Guinea.

● **Right:** Swiss Dr. Kurt Neck is a practicing surgeon and also Council Chairman of Wycliffe in Switzerland.

● **Far right, top and bottom:** Medical doctor Peter Wang and wife Bernice, from Hong Kong, live in Dallas, Texas, where they receive training for translation work.

Many are asking, "Who can show us any good?" Let the light of your face shine upon us, O Lord.

PSALM 4:6

● **Overleaf:** In Suriname, Naomi Glock helps boys read a Saramaccan booklet.

Naomi and her co-workers translated the Saramaccan New Testament. After 23 years on that task, she is now working on a project presenting Old Testament stories in pictorial form with captions in the Saramaccan language.

BOB MANTELL

101

In Suriname, a booklet translated into Saramaccan captures the interest of readers and on-lookers alike.

Who cares if you don't have the real thing? Saramaccan youth in Suriname create their own Checkers game.

Pilot Doug Baughman in Brazil (where he grew up with Wycliffe parents), shoots the breeze with Chief Joaquim.

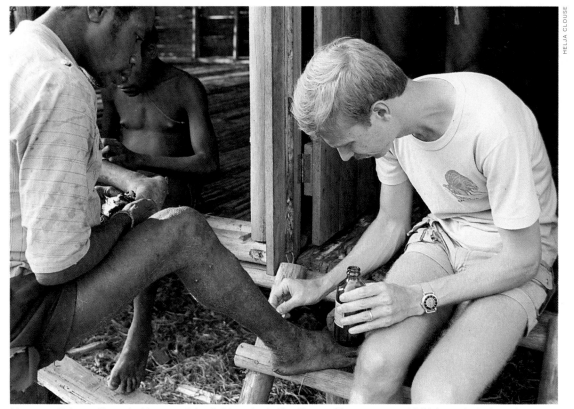

Have medicine, will apply. It's part of the field worker's life. Duane Clouse treats a Kirikiri man in Indonesia.

HAZEL PALILEO

ERIC BINDER

DEBORAH CROUGH

JON ARENSEN

JEANNE ZAUGG

DEBORAH CROUGH

Training is rigorous and thorough for workers going overseas.

● **Far left, top:** After a demonstration on how to build a fire with local materials, trainee Bev Roth attempts her own. This is part of the Field Training Course in Texas preparing Beth for life in Mexico.

● **Far left, middle:** Renowned linguist Dr. Ken Pike has long trained future Bible translators. He also travels internationally, representing SIL and delivering lectures and seminars to translators and the secular linguistic community. At home in Dallas, he works on a writing project.

● **Far left, bottom:** Outdoor Program Supervisor Rick Pfizenmaier repairs an oven used in "Jungle Jump-off" in North Carolina—a program that introduces kids and teens to the world of Wycliffe.

● **Left, top:** At Quest, an initial orientation course, seasoned field workers tell new inquirers what Wycliffe is all about.

● **Left, middle:** Trainees in Kenya, eastern Africa, learn how to make and bake bread outdoors. This is part of a course designed to help workers adapt to different cultural settings.

● **Left, bottom:** In Dallas, Texas, the Summer Institute of Linguistics complex provides most of the training for Bible translators. Students come from all parts of the country, study under veteran translators and linguists, then leave to work all over the world.

Right: Often field workers need to learn a language, such as French or Spanish, to function most effectively overseas. Many field workers bound for French-speaking African countries attend the *Ecole Moderne* in Switzerland.

Near right, middle: The SIL school in Singapore trains people from Asia who want to be translators.

Far right, middle: In this simulation of an African council meeting, students in the Intercultural Communications Course (Dallas) observe cultural forces at work in a conflict situation, and how that conflict was handled.

Near right, bottom: In the Philippines, linguistics consultant Rudy Barlaan orients new translators. Dr. Barlaan is a Filipino who participated in a New Testament translation in the Isnag language.

Far right, bottom: Leslie Sandford and Ron Radke met at an orientation course, met again at a linguistics course a few years later and decided they were a match. Their kind of romance occurs regularly in this work!

FRANCIS ZURCHER

S.E. JESUDASON

DEBORAH CROUGH

JOHNNY TENEGRA

DEBORAH CROUGH

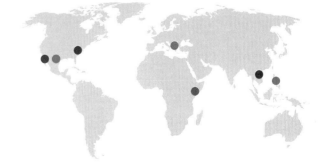

BARB ALVAREZ

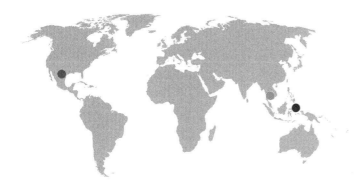

● **Above:** Many minority languages in Asia and the Middle East do have alphabets, but the characters are non-Roman. Problem: how do you reproduce an alphabet like that on a computer that's only made to display Roman letters? Bible translators need specialists to design the characters on computer.

Walter Agee loves to tackle that kind of challenge. In Dallas, Texas, Walt designs a character in the Asian Devanagari script. He takes the character drawn on paper, scans it into his computer, outlines it and cleans it up to meet specifications. Now the computer can reproduce this character on screen and print it out onto paper.

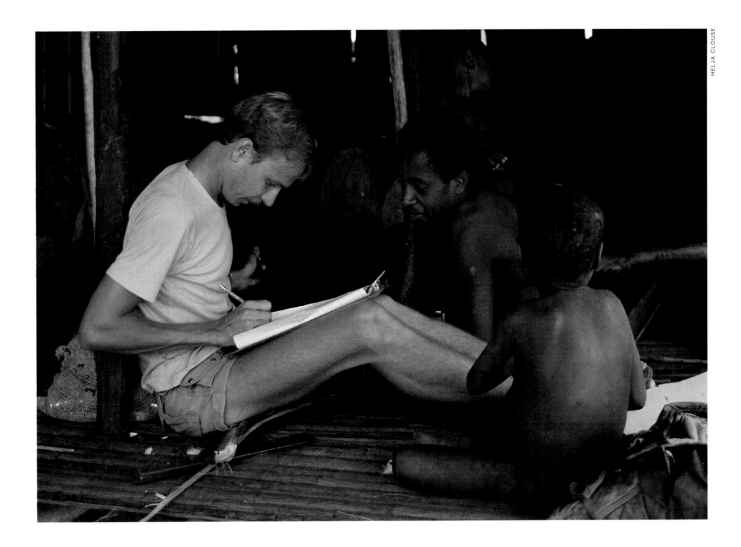

● **Above:** Pencils and paper are still basic tools in language learning and translation. Duane Clouse captures sounds spoken by the Kirikiri people of Indonesia.

● **Left:** While many field personnel work in rural and remote settings, others work in cities, such as Bangkok, Thailand. More and more, rural people are flooding into cities for jobs and education, or to flee war. They still need the Scriptures in their heart languages.

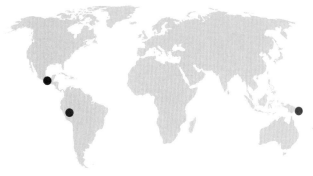

● **Above:** We all need a break sometimes! A little grocery store at SIL's jungle work center in Peru sports a simple snack bar where the "locals" go for a cold Coke in the heat of the day.

● **Top right:** In Mexico, little Timothy Towne finds rest and refuge in his enclosed crib away from flies and mosquitoes. His mom, translator Linda Towne, doesn't mind the moments of quiet between the activities of her busy day.

● **Right:** Nurse Carol Johns (with daughter Becky) treats a baby for malaria. Carol works at the SIL clinic in the highlands of Papua New Guinea, which cares for the health needs of the missionary community and nearby villages.

"Take my yoke upon you and learn from me, for I am gentle and humble in heart, and you will find rest for your souls. For my yoke is easy and my burden is light."

MATTHEW 11:29, 30

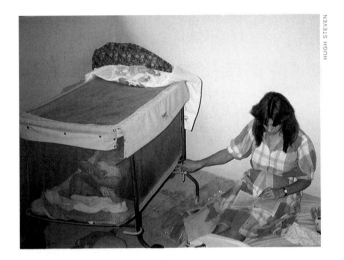

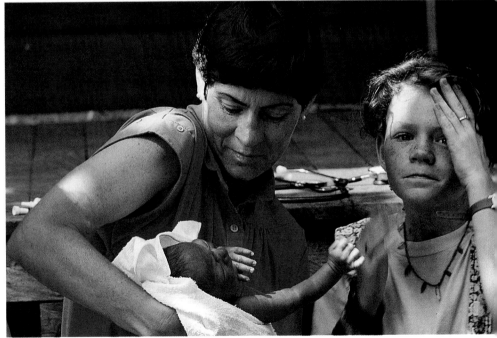

111

LOIS YOUNGMAN

In Indonesia, David Youngman practices a native art: chipping sago pith which will be soaked, squeezed and cooked into the local staple.

At a school for field workers' children in the northern Philippines, third- and fourth-grade kids work on writing drills.

KIRK FRANKLIN

Village friends made the canoe for Brian and Jeremy Clark, sons of Bible translators in Papua New Guinea.

On this Solomon Islands porch, kids naturally build friendships and learn languages, as missionary kids do all over the world.

EDGAR STEPHEN BEACH

In Guatemala, teacher Laurie Welch is part of a worldwide troop that brings quality education to missionary kids such as Isaac Collins.

Kids in Wycliffe-run schools use Macintosh computers for educational programs. This group in the Philippines found the game disk!

● With termite mounds like this to climb on, these boys in eastern Africa could play outside till the ants come home!

Not too many American girls grow up in a place with more monkeys than Barbies, but Sarah Williams does, in Peru.

There's nothing quite like a missionary kid.

Missionary kids (MKs) have a culture all their own. Since they grow up in two or three cultures, they aren't 100 percent like their parents or the people in their adopted country. They get to choose the best from each culture, and have a bigger picture of the whole world.

MKs are unique. Creative. And appreciate individual differences.

Consider their opportunities: MKs get to travel abroad, live close to nature, and see stars undimmed by city lights. They create their own entertainment, learn native crafts from village friends, and grow up blind to skin color. They get an insider's view of another way of life including different kinds of homes, clothes, foods, and ways of thinking. They learn to be independent, responsible and flexible. They receive personal instruction in and out of the classroom. They get to worship God in two or three languages, and watch God touch and change people who have lived in fear of the spirits—and of each other.

Lack of TV, designer jeans or a family car may not be an issue, but leaving home for Middle School or High School isn't easy. Probably their biggest challenge is adjusting to their parents'

home culture when that time comes—often feeling they don't quite fit, and wondering, "Where is home?"

How do MKs feel about being MKs? Roger Jenkins, a computer specialist who grew up in the jungles of Peru, says, "I enjoyed it! I wouldn't trade it for anything. We felt sorry for kids in the States who had to wear shoes all the time! Day in and day out we lived with people who were experts in all kinds of fields—and they always had time for us."

"It's a privilege," says Kim Beaty, a writer who grew up in Papua New Guinea.

An MK and mother of four MKs admits, "It isn't all easy. But is anything worthwhile easy?"

DAVID NICHOLLS

● Winter never comes to Vanuatu—only rainy season. And it's always warm enough for Nathan Garst to enjoy the outdoors.

ALF HOLMAN

● Students who live in remote places, such as Isaac Broad in Australia's outback, talk to teachers in town via two-way radio.

TOM VAN GORKOM

● Wycliffe schools can have student councils and presidents, too. In Colombia, the high school council decides how to use funds.

KIRK FRANKLIN

● Bryan Clark wants to be a helicopter pilot some day. In Papua New Guinea, Bev Preater shows him the ropes.

CLAIRE WAGNER

● MKs sometimes come back to work with Wycliffe as adults. Byron Siemsen, 24, processes receipts at Wycliffe's California office.

ELISABETH JUFER

● This isn't really the way MKs dress. Today is Clash Day at school, and eighth-grader Rebekka Jufer in Brazil is ready!

On a hot, hot day in Australia, what better place to play than a shady concrete culvert?

The Philippines has oodles of treehouse space. If you have a dad handy with a hammer, you're in business.

Many MKs love sports. One can develop formidable skills with hours to practice and no T.V.

Ever had kangaroo-tail stew? Kids such as Celia Broad get to eat all kinds of unusual foods.

KIRK FRANKLIN

● **Above:** Steve Clark has left business management in Chicago with its requisite three-piece suits and jammed traffic. Now a Bible translator in Papua New Guinea, he enjoys the toned-down lifestyle of the village and the purpose in his work. Here Steve and Gwata Andreas search for the cultural parallel of "being bought with the blood of Christ" as they translate 1 Peter into Sio.

Top right: In 1988, Koronas Wajambu was hit by a falling tree, which broke his neck and left him totally paralyzed. During his six-month hospital stay he gave his life to God. He returned to Lambutina village. For the last four years, Dawn Clark, a trained physiotherapist, has given him daily treatment.

Far right: When they're not doing exercises, Dawn and Koronas (left) check the Sio Scripture passages that Steve and Gwata have translated.

KIRK FRANKLIN

● **Previous page and above:** Coconuts, split open and emptied of juice, dry in the sun in Papua New Guinea. After the meat is separated from the husk, it is processed and shipped overseas. The product, called copra, brings little profit because of waning demand in the world market due to high cholesterol content.

KIRK FRANKLIN

That every one may eat and drink, and find satisfaction in all his toil—this is the gift of God.

ECCLESIASTES 3:13

HAZEL LARGE

KIRK FRANKLIN

● **Left:** A portrait of missionary travel, typical except for the smiles! Normally at this stage, the brow furrows, the eyes dart, the mind races. "I know I've forgotten something. . . . Malaria pills? Tickets? Extra battery pack? Film?" But Brian and Celia Bull, from Britain, have years of experience in field travel and packing is old hat to them.

● **Below left:** In Papua New Guinea, Jeanette Bennett washes clothes in a Bamix Presawash (made in Great Britain). It's a cylinder in which clothes rotate in pressurized hot water. Jeanette finds the Presawash ideal for village use since it's small and doesn't require electricity. Daughter Allison enjoys a soak, too.

● **Right:** Rendille man in Kenya, eastern Africa, in a traditional waiting position. It's a fairly typical stance in cultures without chairs.

Cast your cares on the Lord
and he will sustain you.

PSALM 55:22

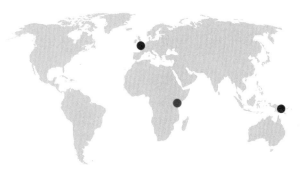

● **Below:** You'll only find kangaroos existing naturally in a few countries. In Australia, a Pitjantjatjara child holds his pet.

LEN WHALLEY

ALF HOLMEN

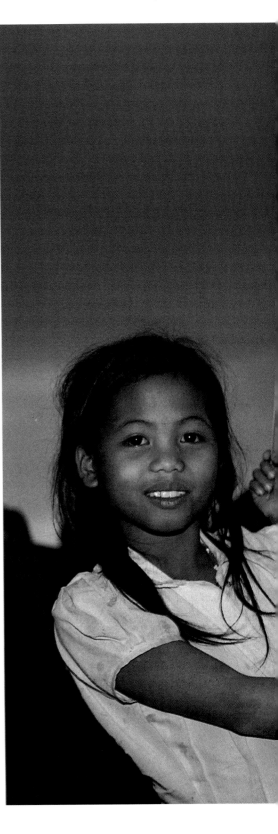

● **Previous page:** In central Australia, where temperatures soar and there's no air-conditioning, translators often work outdoors. With co-worker Bessie Oliver, New Zealanders Neil and Marian Broad study the Eastern Arrernte language.
ALF HOLMEN

● **Above:** In outback Australia, field workers depend on sturdy vehicles to get around—whether to picnic sites or to aboriginal communities for language work.

Now choose life, so that you and your children may live and that you may love the Lord your God, listen to his voice, and hold fast to him.

DEUTERONOMY 30:19, 20

● **Above:** The people who speak the Bambam language live in the mountains of Sulawesi, Indonesia. It takes translators Denise (center) and Phil Campbell twelve hours by bus and three hours on foot to get from the nearest town to the Bambam people. Son Ian (right) is growing up trilingual—he speaks English, Indonesian and Bambam!

ROY HARRIS

ROY HARRIS

ROY HARRIS

ROY HARRIS

● **Top left:** For Ray Rising, Public and Government Relations Officer in Colombia, the job presents lots of variety and some surprises. On this day, a baby boy whom they named Jonathan was abandoned in a box near the SIL community.

Top right: Ray and Asorida, a hospital worker from a nearby town, check Jonathan, who seems healthy. Later he was turned over to a state orphanage, whose staff eventually located his grandparents. Jonathan was released to them.

Above left: Public relations work means time spent with all kinds of people, including kids of local friends.

Above: Visits with national police and government officials are important since field work in this country is carried out with the permission and good graces of those in authority.

Above: The essence of Ray's public relations service is building friend-ships, maintaining con-tacts and representing the work of literacy and Bible translation.

There aren't many flat places among the craggy Finisterre Mountains, but Boksawin Village claims one of them. Homes in this area of Papua New Guinea are made of hand-hewn planks or woven bamboo, thatched with long grass. (**Right**) Swiss Bible translators Urs and Johanna Wegmann work here.

URS WEGMANN

Left: After a passage of Scripture has been translated, it needs to be checked for accuracy and clarity by speakers of the language. Sometimes at this stage only a couple of people do the check; other times a committee is involved. Here a group of Yau men check the book of Acts.

Teach me, O Lord, to follow your decrees;
then I will keep them to the end.

PSALM 119:33

RICK MCARTHUR

● **Far left:** When Guatemalan Bible translator Pedro Bocel isn't at work on the Western Cakchiquel New Testament, he teaches literacy classes. In traditional dress, he rides his motorcycle or walks to Cakchiquel communities in the rugged mountains of Guatemala.

Left: Pedro often finds people enthusiastic about literacy. A prime motivation for literacy frequently is a desire to read God's Word.

Above: Any blank wall will do for taping up a reading drill poster.

TZALU'N NK'AYAJ
TKYAQIL WI Q U'
TOJ ꞁX꞊ TNEJ
Eꞁ TK꞊AQILJO ꞁ
N-AJB'IN TU'N JU
꞊Z'IB'IL EX TU'N
꞊KWELIꞁ..

● **Left:** This bookstore in Guatemala stands as a testimony to the people's pride in their Mam language. Local citizens provided capital to start the store, in which Mam literature is sold. Volunteer staff reproduce books by photocopying and binding on the premises. They sell the books at a high enough price to cover their costs, traveling to markets in the area to sell them. Self-sustaining vernacular bookstores like this are still rare in Central America.

Below: Historically, Guatemalan children were taught exclusively in Spanish. In recent years, some schools have adopted the "vernacular" approach—teaching kids in their native tongue first, then integrating Spanish in higher grades. It has proved to be a successful method, since students don't have to struggle to learn new educational concepts in a foreign language.

One day this little girl, now learning to read in her Mam language, will also be able to read the Scriptures in her language. Perhaps she will use them to encourage others, as does this gentleman for his sick friend (**right**).

Lower right: Pastor José Víctor Pérez was one of the first Christians in the area. He now uses the Mam Scriptures for clear communication as he teaches his growing church.

Rendille elders meet with Nick Swanepoel and co-translators to listen to Scriptures translated in draft form. The verses have been recorded onto cassette, which the men are listening to on a hand-cranked player.

This audio checking session is a way to elicit feedback from those elders who haven't learned to read yet. Their support of the Scripture translation is crucial because they strongly influence Rendille society.

*May the nations be glad and sing for joy, for you . . .
guide the nations of the earth.*

PSALM 67:4

Above: At Makerere
University in Uganda
(eastern Africa), Danish
translation consultant Iver
Larsen gives a lecture on
orthography (spelling
and alphabets).
   Such linguistic work is
foundational to Bible
translation.

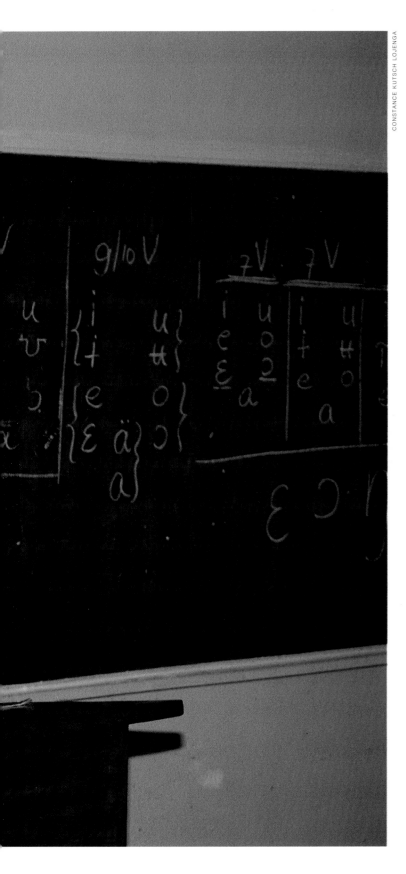

Top: Ron Moe coordinates SIL's work in Uganda, conducts language surveys and lectures at Makerere University.

Middle: Iver Larsen confers with students and African professors at the orthography seminar.

Bottom: Representatives from the Bible Society of Uganda attended the seminar to receive training.

In Peru, a woman makes her way upriver, using the basic form of transportation her people have depended on for centuries. So often, these people who live close to the heartbeat of nature with the barest of essentials speak languages of great complexity and intricacy.

This translation **(Inset)** in the Nomatsiguenga language gives fresh insight into the far-reaching effects of Babel many centuries ago.

Large photo: In the Bontoc area of the Philippines, interest runs high in producing vernacular literature.

Australian Bible translator Keith Benn and translator committee member Khensay pick their way through paddies to a meeting with local officials about new health books written in the Bontoc language.

Below: Eduardo Yañgo checks for accuracy in the translation of Romans. He's part of the Bontoc Translation Committee (**bottom**), meeting here in the Benns' house. Suited up for the occasion, they discuss the revisions made earlier on the translation of Romans.

K.J. KENFIELD

K.J. KENFIELD

JUNE HATHERSMITH

● **Above:** "When my husband travels long distances and sends me a letter, I can read it for myself." Rendille women of eastern Africa who are learning to read see many benefits to literacy. "When I go to the store, I can't be cheated. . . . At the hospital, I can sign my name instead of just putting my mark."

Right: Rendille elders and warriors also attend literacy classes. Their enthusiasm gives reading a status and influences younger men to learn to read, too.

He has made everything beautiful in its time. He has also set eternity in the hearts of men; yet they cannot fathom what God has done from beginning to end.

ECCLESIASTES 3:11

● **Above:** In the foreground stand some of the pillars of Wycliffe. These have each contributed at least 40 years of service and have helped establish a ministry that is continuing into the future—a ministry that the building behind them will help to forward.

Standing, left to right: Don Olson, Evelyn and Ken Pike, Don Stark, Faith and Dick Blight, Ruth Stark, Ethel and Frank Robbins, Wayne and Betty Snell, Clarence and Katherine Church.

Seated, left to right: Anne Olson, Eunice Pike, Alfa Curtis, Marianna Slocum, Florence Gerdel, Vola Griste, Elaine Beekman, Olive Shell, Martha Philips, Iris and Alan Wares.

These folks have helped construct Wycliffe Bible Translators. The Wycliffe Associates (WA) crew in the background is doing the same thing, but with physical materials.

Left to right: Bob Hoover, Roger Bostick, George Carnevale, Kenneth Pagel, Louis Roossien and Steve Cowles are constructing the international administration building in Dallas.

WA work crews are staffed predominantly by volunteers.

WYCLIFFE
ASSOCIATES
CONSTRUCTI
MINISTRIE

● **Top**: Bible translator and literacy specialist Faith Hill began linguistic work back in the '40s. With co-workers, she translated the Navajo and Apache New Testaments. She has also worked in Israel, Australia, the Middle East, and Tucson, Arizona.

● **Above**: In Burkina Faso, West Africa, Elsie Badoun (standing) teaches women to read in their Karaboro language.

When your words came, I ate them; they were my joy and my heart's delight.

JEREMIAH 15:16

● **Left and below:** In a bright, busy marketplace in Togo, West Africa, Swedish translator Helene Boethius sells Ife-language literature. (Can you spot her?) The translated materials include stories of the good Samaritan and the birth of Christ, an alphabet book and a book of traditional Ife riddles.

Short, interesting books help whet people's appe-tites for more, and often entice illiterates to learn to read. They're sold at a cost low enough so people can afford them, yet high enough that they represent something of worth.

Promoting translated materials is just part of Helene's job. Her main task is working with co-translators to put the Scriptures into Ife.

● **Right:** If you have to portage, this is one way to go. Actually, Neel and Lane Carpenter won't canoe a whole lot here in the highlands of Papua New Guinea, where SIL's work center is located. They've just returned from a visit to the coastal village where they lived for part of their field training. An adopted father made the canoe for them.

● **Below:** In Indonesia, translator Duane Clouse records Kirikiri words in a language-learning session with a friend. Also an ethnomusicologist (one who studies the music of non-European cultures), Duane began work here recently with his Finnish wife, Helja.

*Our mouths were filled with laughter, our tongues with
songs of joy. Then it was said among the nations,
"The Lord has done great things for them."*

PSALM 126:2

DAVID ANDERSEN

● **Above:** Oops! Translator Suree Andersen (right) just made a language blooper. In this language-learning business, you have to dive in head first, try to talk, be willing to make mistakes and then laugh at them. Otherwise frustration and a sense of failure can do you in. Suree, from Thailand, and her Australian husband, David, are plunging in to the Moronene language of Indonesia, for which they hope to translate the Scriptures.

BOB MANTELL

All nations will come and worship before you, for your righteous acts have been revealed.

REVELATION 15:4

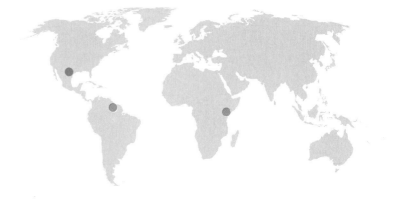

● **Left:** Carmen Asoedanoe is a Saramaccan from Suriname. She knows how to read and write, and now has the Scriptures in her own language.

● **Right:** Morris and Wendy Johnson, in Dallas, are training to be Bible translators. Initially, they worked in Papua New Guinea, Morris as an aircraft mechanic. But as they saw the great need for Bible translators in that country of over 800 languages, they decided to change careers.

Morris works on grammatical analysis at his home computer while Wendy and daughter Rachel watch.

● **Below:** It's time to kick back and relax as a family.

DEBORAH CROUGH

DEBORAH CROUGH

● **Overleaf:** At day's end in Kenya, eastern Africa, Rendille warriors herd their camels and cattle toward a thorn-bush corral. As they keep vigil over the animals and watch for lions, they pass the night by telling stories, singing "clan songs" and drinking *chai*—tea, milk and sugar boiled together.

JUNE HATHERSMITH

> *Listen, listen to me, and eat what is good,*
> *and your soul will delight in the richest of fare.*
>
> ISAIAH 55:2

◔ On St. Lawrence Island in Alaska, Mitzi Shinen serves husband Dave reindeer stew.

◔ Food and fellowship with Ron and Beth Moe (at right) in Kampala, Uganda, beats the "Golden Arches" any day.

◔ Little Maia Severn, daughter of British Bible translators John and Lois in Indonesia, joins in saying "grace."

◔ Paul Eckert (left) and David Crawford tend to the barbecue on an outing with their families in central Australia.

RICK KROWCHENKO

Henny Leonard stirs the chicken in Kenya, eastern Africa. She's just visiting in a Sabaot friend's home and making herself useful.

RUSS PERRY

Pat Andrews enjoys the cuisine of a local hotel in Indonesia during his survey trip to determine where to work in Bible translation.

PETE LAWRY

Kim and Carolyn Fowler eat their dinner by candlelight. There's no electricity in this jungle area of Potaya, Peru.

ALF HOLMEN

Extra onions, please. In Australia, Neil and Marian Broad (from New Zealand) and daughter Celia get ready for a pizza feast.

Overleaf: In Guatemala, Cakchiquel Indians have gathered to sing and watch a video based on the book of Luke. The script has been dubbed into their native southern Cakchiquel language.

RICK MCARTHUR

In Alaska, Dave and Mitzi Shinen work on translation revisions on the Yupik Scriptures.

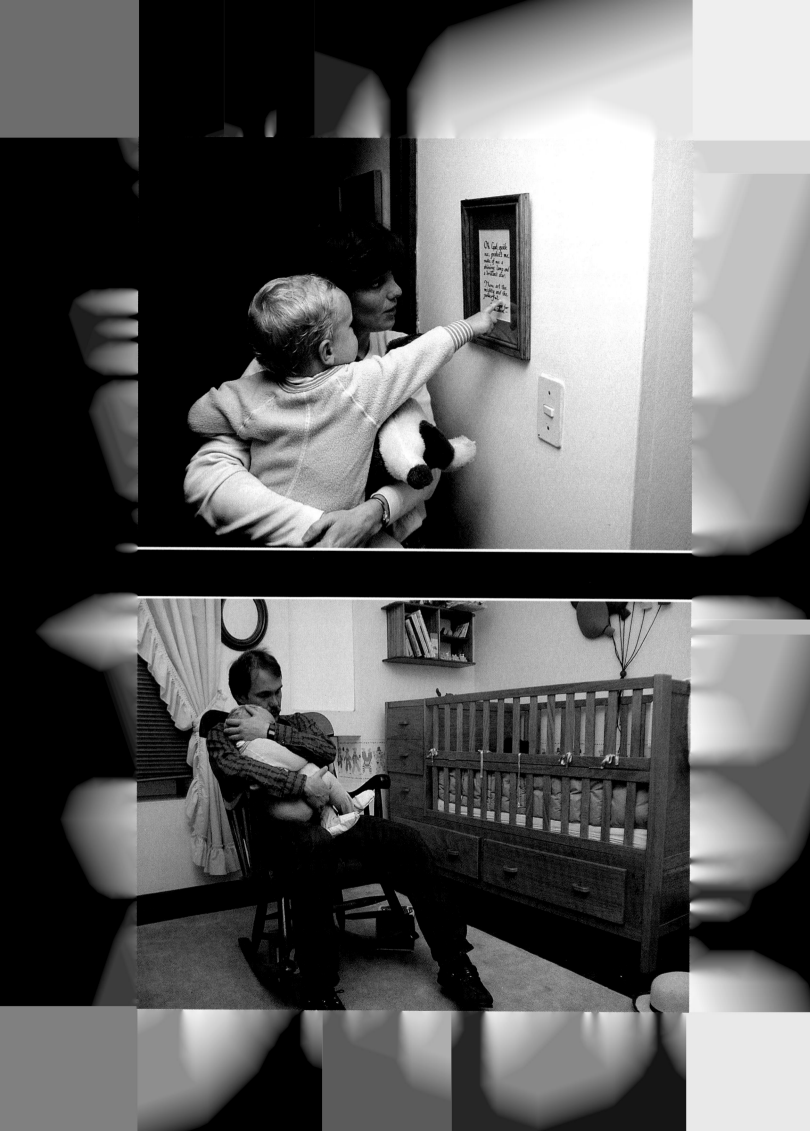

*I will lie down and sleep in peace,
for you alone, O Lord, make me
dwell in safety.*

PSALM 4:8

Left and above: Daylight has long faded, and as the quiet of night descends, evening rituals unfold around the world. In the Moore household in Lima, Peru, little Andrew gets cuddled by mom Kathryn, rocked by dad Steve, and then sneaks a peek during prayer time.

Andrew is a second-generation MK; his dad was also raised in Peru as the son of missionaries. Steve speaks fluent Spanish, an asset of inestimable value in his work in government relations.

Jeremy Kaetterhenry winds down the day in Australia with a good book.

In Papua New Guinea, pilot Bev Preater checks maps to determine tomorrow's flight plan.

The mighty One, God, the Lord, speaks and summons the earth from the rising of the sun to the place where it sets.

PSALM 50:1

Alan Rogers works on labels for cassettes of Garawa Scripture songs in Australia.

Terry Van Gorkom in Colombia prays for protection and peaceful sleep for little Jessica.

163

. . . there before me was a great multitude that no one could count, from every nation, tribe, people and language, standing before the throne and in front of the Lamb.

REVELATION 7:9

Great joy and celebration mark any New Testament dedication. Though this one occurred on a day other than October 1, it represents the dedications that take place around the world over a dozen times per year.

At this dedication of the Sepik Iwam Scriptures, a pastor held up a bone knife — a common weapon among the Sepik Iwam people in former days. "We are celebrating another powerful weapon today," the pastor said. "But as the knife is powerless unless you pick it up and use it, the Bible is worthless unless you pick it up, read it and use it."

165

New Testament translations completed
by members of Wycliffe Bible Translators and local partners. Listed by
country in order of completion, followed
by number of speakers.

*Parentheses ( ) indicate a particular language
dialect. Brackets [ ] indicate alternative
language names.*

AUSTRALIA
Pintupi-Luritja, 800
Kuku-Yalanji, 600
Walmajarri, 800
Wik-Mungkan, 1,000
Burarra, 600
Kriol, 20,000

BENIN, Western Africa
Fon, 1,030,000

BOLIVIA, South America
Guarani (Eastern), 35,000
Quechua (Sucre), 2,782,500
Siriono, 500
Chipaya, 1,000
Chacobo, 250
Chiquitano, 20,000
Ignaciano, 5,000
Tacana, 5,000
Ese Ejja, 1,000
Guarani (Western), 5,000
Cavinena, 2,000
Guarayu, 5,000
Quechua (Northern Bolivia), 100,000

BRAZIL, South America
Hixkaryana, 250
Kaingang, 10,500
Munduruku, 2,000
Maxakali, 270
Palikur, 1,000
Karaja, 2,400
Guajajara, 6,000
Satare-Mawe, 5,000
Kaiwa, 12,000
Apalai, 350
Urubu Kaapor, 500
Guarani, 3,000
Canela, 2,500
Kayapo, 2,200
Nambikuara (Southern), 700
Tenharim, 250
Terena, 15,000

CAMEROON, Central Africa
Fali (South), 20,000
Mandara, 43,000
Zulgo, 18,000
Tikar, 20,000
Nso, 120,000
Doyayo, 18,000
Yamba, 25,000

COLOMBIA, South America
Paez, 40,000
Muinane, 200
Guahibo, 20,000
Guanano, 800
Siona, 300
Yucuna, 800
Desano, 1,000
Witoto, 2,500
Tatuyo, 400
Piapoco, 3,000
Cuiba, 2,000
Tunebo (Central), 3,000
Tucano, 5,000
Macuna, 450
Cubeo, 4,000
Camsa, 4,000
Piratapuyo, 1,070
Carapana, 350
Koreguaje, 2,000

CÔTE D'IVOIRE, Western Africa
Toura, 25,000
Bete (Western), 350,000
Wobe, 100,000
Nyabwa, 30,000
Dan [Yacouba], 350,000

ECUADOR, South America
Shuar, [Jivaro] 32,000
Cofan, 700
Colorado, 1,800
Secoya, 500
Waorani [Auca], 800
Quichua (Pastaza), 4,000

ETHIOPIA, Eastern Africa
Gedeo, 500,000
Gimira, 50,000

GHANA, Western Africa
Kusaal, 188,000
Konkomba, 340,000
Vagla 7,000
Tampulma, 8,000
Hanga, 4,000
Nafaanra, 35,000
Sisaala (Tumulung), 80,000
Bimoba, 70,000
Frafra, 450,000
Kasem, 85,000
Chumburung, 16,000

GUATEMALA, Central America
Chuj (San Sebastian Coatan), 16,000
Aguatec, 20,000
Quiche (Central), 210,000
Mopan Maya, 2,000
Cakchiquel (Central), 126,000
K'anjobal (Acatan), 15,000
Tzutujil, 50,000
Carib (Black), 70,000
Achi (Cubulco), 18,000
Cakchichel (Eastern), 100,000
Cakchichel (Southwestern), 8,000
Kekchi, 283,000

INDIA
Kupia, 6,000

INDONESIA
Berik, 1,000

MALAYSIA
Tagal Murut, 16,000

MEXICO
Mixteco (San Miguel), 4,000
Tzeltal (Highland), 25,000
Totonaco (Highland), 120,000
Chol (Tumbala), 50,000
Mazateco (Highland), 60,000
Tzeltal (Bachajon), 20,000
Huichol, 12,000
Zoque (Copainala), 6,000
Trique (San Andres), 6,000
Chinanteco (Ojitlan), 10,000
Popoluca (Sayula), 6,000
Tarasco, 60,000
Mazahua, 400,000
Otomi (Mezquital), 100,000
Zapoteco (Sierra Juarez), 3,000
Huasteco (San Luis Potosi), 39,000
Zapoteco (Miahuatlan), 80,000
Zapoteco (Northern Villa Alta) [Rincon],
  15,000
Zapoteco (Yatzachi), 3,000
Cuicateco (Teutila), 20,000
Huave, 12,000
Tarahumara (Samachique), 40,000
Tojolabal, 14,000
Zapoteco (Isthmus), 75,000
Amuzgo (Guerrero), 25,000
Chinanteco (Palantla), 11,000
Mixteco (Atatlahuca), 8,000

Chinanteco (Lalana), 10,000
Cuicateco (Tepeuxila), 2,500
Otomi (Eastern), 20,000
Otomi (Mexico State), 7,000
Otomi (Tenango), 10,000
Tzotzil (Huixtan), 7,000
Chol (Tila), 40,000
Mixe (Coatlan), 5,000
Tepehua (Huehuetla), 3,000
Chontal (Tabasco), 40,000
Mixteco (Ocotepec), 8,000
Popoluca (Highland), 25,000
Yaqui, 25,000
Lacandon, 550
Mixteco (Southern Puebla), 3,000
Totonaco (Northern), 80,000
Zoque (Francisco Leon), 5,000
Mixteco (Chayuco), 30,000
Mixteco (Penoles), 14,000
Nahuatl (Sierra), 125,000
Nahuatl (North Puebla), 60,000
Totonaco (Papantla), 80,000
Tzotzil (Chamula), 50,000
Mixe (Juquila), 8,500
Chinanteco (Lealao), 1,000
Mixteco (Western Jamiltepec), 15,000
Nahuatl (Tetelcingo), 3,000
Chatino (Tataltepec), 2,500
Tepehuan (Northern), 5,000
Tzotzil (Chenalho), 11,000
Zapoteco (Mitla), 15,000
Zapoteco, (Central Villa Alta) [Tabaa], 1,500
Popoloca (Eastern), 2,000
Seri, 600
Chinanteco (Quiotepec), 10,000
Tzotzil (San Andres), 30,000
Chinanteco (Usila), 10,000
Mixteco (Eastern Jamiltepec), 30,000
Popoloca (Northern), 5,000
Nahuatl (Eastern Huastec), 300,000
Zapoteco (Ocotlan), 20,000
Chinanteco (Sochiapan), 4,000
Zapoteco (Choapan), 20,000
Nahuatl (Western Huasteco), 300,000
Tzotzil (Zinacanteco), 10,000
Nahuatl (Central), 100,000
Totonaco (Coyutla), 30,000
Zapoteco (Zoogocho), 1,300
Mixteco (Yosondua), 15,000
Mixe (Tlahuitoltepec), 15,000
Trique (Copala), 8,000
Mixe (Guichicovi), 18,000
Zapoteco (Texmelucan), 3,000
Zapoteco (Chichicapan), 8,000
Mixe (Totontepec), 5,000
Mazateco (Chiquihuitlan), 4,000
Chontal (Highland), 5,000
Amuzgo (Oaxaca), 7,500

NIGERIA, Western Africa
Ekajuk, 15,000
Kamwe [Higi], 180,000
Engenni, 20,000
Mambila, 60,000
Angas, 100,000
Longuda, 32,000
Abua, 24,000
Dghwede, 16,000
Ezaa, 180,000
Igede, 70,000
Ikwo, 150,000
Izi, 200,000
Ebira, 500,000
Kaje, 52,000
Bekwarra, 60,000
Berom, 200,000
Mbembe (Cross River), 100,000
Migili, 50,000
Tarok, 140,000

PANAMA, Central America
Wounaan, 6,000
Buglere, 3,000

PAPUA NEW GUINEA
Kewa (West), 25,000
Yareba, 750
Awa, 1,800
Daga, 5,500
Fore, 17,000
Alekano, [Gahuku], 16,500
Kwoma, [Washkuk], 3,000
Guhu-Samane, 6,500
Iatmul, 12,000
Managalasi, 5,000
Siroi, 700
Waffa, 1,000
Wantoat, 7,500
Fasu, 1,200
Muyuw, 3,000
Kamano-Kafe, 50,000
Buang (Central), 7,000
Halia, 14,000
Salt-Yui, 6,500
Suena, 2,500
Manambu, 2,100
Tairora, 13,300
Golin, 51,200
Kanite, 15,000
Komba, 12,300
Kosena (Auyaana), 4,500
Nii, 9,300
Usarufa, 2,000
Yessan-Mayo, 1,000
Buang (Mangga), 3,000
Gadsup, 12,000
Mt. Koiali, 3,700
Narak, 5,000
Bena-Bena, 16,000
Au, 5,000
Rotokas, 4,200
Yaweyuha, 2,000
Zia, 5,000
Ambulas, 8,500
Iduna, 6,000
Binumarien, 267
Nakanai, 10,000
Awiyaana, 2,000
Iamalele, 3,000
Iwal, 1,500
Uri 2,500
Weri, 4,200
Biangai, 4,000
Tawala, 10,000
Korafe, 3,000
Dobu, 100,000
Waskia, 12,000
Mianmin, 1,700
Patep, 1,700
Selepet, 7,000
Ewage, 12,000
Rossel, 3,300
Dadibi, 12,000
Timbe, 11,000
Telefol, 5,000
Aneme Wake, 650
Mufian, 5,500
Orokaiva, 25,000
Kunimaipa, 10,000
Nobonob, 2,000
Sepik Iwam, 1,500
Upper Asaro, 30,000
Ampeeli, 1,100
Ama, 400
Angave, 900
Bunama, 1,500
Bukiyip, 10,300
Chuave, 23,100
Kalam, 14,000
Oksapmin, 7,000
Omie, 1,100
Ono, 5,400
Siane, 18,000

PERU, South America
Piro, 2,500
Campa (Ashaninca), 18,000
Aguaruna, 25,000

Huambisa, 6,000
Machiguenga, 8,000
Amuesha, 8,000
Chayahuita, 6,000
Cashibo, 1,500
Huitoto (Murui), 1,500
Candoshi, 3,000
Campa (Nomatsiguenga), 2,500
Capanahua, 500
Cashinahua, 3,000
Achuar, 5,000
Quechua (Ayacucho), 900,000
Bora, 3,000
Amarakaeri, 500
Ticuna, 25,000
Arabela, 300
Quechua (Pastaza), 2,000

PHILIPPINES
Mansaka, 35,000
Dumagat (Umiray), 5,000
Ifugao (Batad), 43,000
Manobo (Western Bukidnon), 15,000
Ibaloi, 88,000
Tboli, 80,000
Dumagat (Casiguran) [Agta], 1,000
Ifugao, Anganad, 4,000
Ifugao (Antipolo), 5,000
Isnag, 10,000
Blaan (Sarangani), 150,000
Chavacano, 200,000
Manobo (Dibabawon), 10,000
Balangao, 5,000
Mamanwa, 1,500
Manobo (Sarangani), 30,000
Sambal (Botolan), 20,000
Tiruray, 35,000
Ivatan, 30,000
Tausug, 400,000
Yakan, 60,000
Kankanay (Northern), 60,000
Bunukid, 100,000
Sama (Central) 100,000
Kalinga (Southern), 11,000
Ibanag, 500,000
Manobo (Ilianen), 10,000
Manobo (Cotobato), 12,000
Caluyanun, 20,000
Kankanaey, 150,000
Ifugao (Tuwali), 20,000
Masbatenyo, 333,000
Tagbanwa, 8,000

SOUTH ASIA
Gurung (Western), 90,000
Kham, 40,000
Newari, 500,000
Magar (Eastern), 500,000

SURINAME, South America
Saramaccan, 20,000

TOGO, Western Africa
Ntcham [Bassar], 48,000

UNITED STATES
Navaho, 130,000
Apache (Western), 11,000
Eskimo (Inupiat), 4,000
Hopi, 5,000
Papago-Pima, 15,000
Paiute (Northern), 2,000
Plautdietsch (Low German), 80,000

VIETNAM
Bahnar, 85,000
Katu, 30,000
Bru, 50,000
Chrau, 20,000

ZAIRE, Central Africa
Ngbaka, 750,000

Organizations and individuals who underwrote the publishing costs for one or more New Testaments listed on these pages:

Bible Society of Australia

Bible Society of Papua New Guinea

The Bible League (formerly World Home Bible League)

International Bible Society

Bible Society of Ethiopia

Nigeria Bible Translation Trust

United Bible Societies

Kristen Press (Papua New Guinea)

Philippines Bible Society

Kindred Press

Bible Society of Mexico

Ivoirian Bible Translation Association

Wycliffe Bible Translators

Dr. Kurt Koch (Germany)

Looney Foundation

Bible Society of Nigeria

Bible Society of Zaire

World Literature Crusade

Park Press

Wycliffe Associates

American Bible Society

Editora Sinodal (Brazil)

Livraria Crista Unida (Brazil)

Bible Society of Guatemala

Tipografia Indigena (Mexico, publishers of first SIL translation in 1951)

. . .my word that goes out from my mouth. . .will not return to me empty, but will accomplish what I desire and achieve the purpose for which I sent it.

ISAIAH 55:11

HUGH STEVEN

● Doug Towne in Mexico takes a last look at the translated portions of Mark he and co-translator Pascual worked on today. Soon Doug will head for bed. Tomorrow comes soon, bringing another day of friendship-building, language-learning and translating the Word of God for a people who have never had it before.